Discursive analytical strategies

Understanding Foucault, Koselleck, Laclau, Luhmann

Niels Åkerstrøm Andersen

First published in Great Britain in January 2003 by

The Policy Press
Fourth Floor, Beacon House
Queen's Road
Bristol BS8 1QU
UK

Tel +44 (0)117 331 4054
Fax +44 (0)117 331 4093
e-mail tpp-info@bristol.ac.uk
www.policypress.org.uk

British Library Cataloguing in Publication Data

A catalogue record for this book is available from the British Library

ISBN 978 1 86134 439 7 paperback

A hardcover version of this book is also available

Niels Åkerstrøm Andersen is Professor of Political Management at the Department of
Management, Politics and Philosophy, Copenhagen Business School, Denmark.

Cover design by Qube Design Associates, Bristol.

Front cover: photograph supplied by kind permission of Mary Shaw.

Printed and bound in Great Britain by Marston Book Services, Oxford.

Contents

List of tables and figures   IV

Acknowledgements   V

Glossary   VI

Introduction   IX

1   The discourse analysis of Michel Foucault   1

2   Reinhart Koselleck's history of concepts   33

3   The discourse theory of Ernesto Laclau   49

4   Niklas Luhmann's systems theory   63

5   A hall of mirrors or a pool of analytical strategies   93

References   119

Appendix A: Examples of other analytical strategies   125

Appendix B: Further reading   127

Index   131

List of tables and figures

Tables

0.1	Method versus analytical strategy	XIII
1.1	Foucault's analytical strategies	31
2.1	Koselleck's analytical strategies	48
3.1	Laclau's analytical strategies	62
4.1	First- versus second-order observation	71
4.2	The differentiation of society	83
4.3	Luhmann's analytical strategies	92
5.1	Analytical strategies compared	97
5.2	Problems of conditioning related to the analytical strategies	114

Figures

1.1	The genealogy of psychoanalysis	21
1.2	The elements of self-technology	25
1.3	Dispositive analysis	28
1.4	The double movement of dispositive analysis	29
2.1	Synchronous versus diachronic	47
3.1	Chains of difference and equivalence	55
3.2	The relationship between deconstruction and discourse analysis	58
4.1	The sign of difference	65
4.2	The marked difference	65
4.3	A difference observed through a difference	66
4.4	The distinction system/environment re-entered as a part of itself	67
4.5	The sign of re-entry	68
4.6	Re-entry of the distinction system/environment	81
4.7	The calculus of form	84
4.8	Media/form staircase	86
4.9	The relationship between form analysis and semantic analysis	89
4.10	The relationship between differentiation and semantics	90
4.11	The relationship between systems analysis and media analysis	91
5.1	Analytical strategy	117

Acknowledgements

This book presents Michel Foucault, Reinhart Koselleck, Ernesto Laclau and Niklas Luhmann as analytical strategists. There is a reason for this. I have for some years been studying the more fundamental changes in European societies. Trying to capture these fundamental changes, it is easy to become a victim of current self-descriptions and future images in society. Instead of grasping the changes you become a prisoner of the discourse producers of the day and their strategically constructed future images. It is easy to confuse the actual changes with the images and, in so doing, one may become an instrument in confirming the discourse producers' political predictions of trends: globalisation, the knowledge society, the network society and the dream society. Studying change, it is essentially difficult to maintain the necessary distance to the object; to the society that should be studied.

In my terminology, this problem is one of analytical strategy: how can you critically analyse a coherence of meaning of which you are a part? Foucault, Koselleck, Laclau and Luhmann explored this problem and it is the four very different strategies of handling it that form the theme of this book.

The book has been written in a very inspiring environment at the Department of Management, Politics and Philosophy at Copenhagen Business School. I would like to thank my colleagues for their challenging discussions and fruitful comments. In particular I would like to thank Christina Thyssen, Asmund Born and Hanne Knudsen.

Glossary

An *analytical strategy* is a second-order strategy for the observation of how 'the social' emerges in observations (or enunciations and articulations). The elaboration of an analytical strategy involves shaping a specific gaze that allows the environment to appear as consisting of the observations of other people or systems.

Communication is a selection process, consisting of a synthesis of three selections: (1) selection of information, that is, what is to be communicated; (2) selection of form of message, that is, how the information is to be communicated; and finally, (3) selection of understanding, that is, what should be understood about the message.

Concept (Koselleck) is a word condensing a wide range of social and political meanings. Concepts comprise an undecided abundance of meaning, a concentration of meaning, which makes them ambiguous. Precisely through its ambiguity, the concept creates a space of signification, which is open to interpretation and can become a semantic battlefield.

Deconstruction is showing how differences are contingent, that is, deconstruction is about retracting or unpacking differences to show that they are not differences at all – that the 'bar' (/) between two opposing elements, which isolates one from the other, cannot be maintained. In short, to deconstruct is to demonstrate the impossibility of a distinction.

Discourse (Foucault), or more precisely a discursive formation, is a system of dispersion for statements. It is not a structure existing on a level different from statements; discursive formation is simply the regularity of the irregular distribution of statements.

Discourse (Laclau) is a structural totality of differences that is a result of an articulatory practice. The totality is, however, never fully achieved. Discourse is a never-completed fixation process that takes place through articulation within a field of discoursivity with drifting relations.

Form (Luhmann) is the unity of a difference.

A *guiding distinction* is the distinction that can define the frame for second-order observations. For the second-order observer, the guiding distinction divides the world and dictates how the world can be observed.

Hegemony is only possible when something exists that can be *hegemonised*. This only occurs when a discourse lacks final fixation, when the discursive elements hold a surplus of meaning, and when the signifiers are not irreversibly linked to the signified. Consequently, hegemony signifies the never-concluded attempts to produce a fixed point of discourse, to which there will always be a threat.

Information is a difference that makes a difference to a system. It is the system itself that selects information from pure noise and irritation on the basis of its own operation of distinction. That is, the system needs expectations to be surprised.

Method is the rules and procedures required to produce scientific knowledge.

Nodal points are privileged discursive points, which serve to arrest the flow of relationships without ever becoming a real centre of the discourse. The discursive struggle about the construction of nodal points is, so to speak, a struggle about the conditions of conflicts within a specific discourse.

Re-entry is the operation by which a difference is copied into itself, thus becoming a part of itself.

Second-order observation is an observation of an observation as an observation. That is, not reducing an observation to something else, for example, to an ideology, individual intentions, subjectivity and so on. An observation is an indication within a frame of difference.

Semantics (Luhmann) are characterised as the accumulated amount of generalised forms of differences (for example, concepts, ideas, images and symbols) available for the selection of meaning within systems of communication.

Social system is an autopoietic system of communication, which defines itself in the construction of its environment through communicative descriptions. A social system is a system only in relation to its environment, and the environment, in turn, exists only in relation to a system. Both system and environment are internal structures of communication. However, environment is not 'reality' as such. Environment consists of that which is defined by the communication as its relevant surroundings. Any system therefore is identical to itself in its difference (and only in its difference) from the internal environment construction.

Statement is a function of existence that enables groups of signs to exist. The statement is the smallest unit, which brings forth phenomenon through enunciation. We are therefore able to recognise the statement by its momentary creation rather than by its appearance as sign, sentence, book or argument. Statements are positive events that produce existence through enunciation. This function of existence contains at least four aspects: object, subject, conceptual network and strategy.

Subject positions are the spaces from which one speaks and observes in a discursive formation. Subject positions have rules for the acceptance of certain individuals into the spaces, rules for acceptance regarding in what situation the subject position can be used as a platform for speaking and observing, and rules for the formation of statements once one has assumed a specific position.

Subjecting indicates that an individual or a collective is proclaimed to be a subject within a specific discourse. The individual or the collective is offered a particular position in the discourse from which they can speak and act in a meaningful way. Subjecting thus signifies the space in which the discursive individual *receives itself*.

Subjectivation happens when the individual or the collective is not only formed as a subject but also *wishes to be* the subject. Subjectivation signifies the space in which the individual *gives itself to itself*.

Introduction

From method to analytical strategy

The social sciences currently exist in the light of constructivism. A number of social scientists see themselves as different types of constructivists, and the constructivist spectrum is broad – from Peter Berger and Thomas Luckmann via Pierre Bourdieu to Michel Foucault and Niklas Luhmann. So, why is constructivism so popular now? In my view it has simply become too difficult not to be a constructivist. Regardless of the field of social science one focuses on, the most noticeable thing is change, and changes often touch upon and challenge fundamental values, raising questions about the constituent character of what we see.

If we look at politics, the European nation states are being integrated in the European Union and the World Trade Organisation – a process that challenges the value of the sovereign state. If we look at medicine, new technologies (such as prenatal diagnosis) question the value of individuality. The welfare state is experiencing a growing number of reforms based on spending politics, which questions the value of solidarity. We frequently find that our categories do not suffice; they seem inadequate. They appear to point to a former order of society that no longer exists. This is the case with, for example, the notion of state sovereignty. We use the 'conventional concept' to evaluate the concept's change. We evaluate European integration by using categories belonging to a dated world order. We analyse the future by the standards of the past.

Our experiences of the insufficiency of categories encourage us to take a step back in order to look at the categories themselves – their construction, their history and their position within the fields of our focus. Rather than analysing European integration from the perspective of 'state sovereignty', we inquire about the concept of sovereignty itself and the historical conditions of its existence and transformation. We inquire into how the idea of the sovereign state has been shaped and how it may be threatened by the European Union. We look at which new concepts could be emerging, which new meanings the old concept of sovereignty is given, how a new institutionalised framework is built around a new understanding of sovereignty and so on. Rather than forming an immediate judgement of new technologies, we make inquiries about the evolution of technology and of individual values. In what way do new technologies change our understanding of life, individuality, destiny, responsibility and freedom? To what extent do new technologies not only create new ideas, but also revive old ideas and reopen old questions, for example the question of social hygiene dating back to the social reforms of the 1920s and 1930s?

At the same time, knowledge has become an intrinsic part of the organisation of society in a much more strategic way than before. Today sociologists speak of the knowledge society, the corporate community talks about knowledge management. Generating knowledge is no longer exclusive to independent scientific institutions such as universities. In the corporate community, knowledge-intensive businesses have been established, such as the big international consulting firms PLS Consult, Deloitte & Touche and McKinsey. They do not simply operate and utilise organisation theories developed by the universities. They are themselves generators of theories and concepts, and their concept development not only serves the purpose of scientific knowledge, it also aims to seduce and sell.

Within government, similar discursive institutions have been established in order to develop scientific discourses and to diagnose the condition of society, with the intention of controlling the political agenda, defining the framework for negotiation and installing a sense of responsibility in organisations, political parties and individuals. One European example is the European Environment Agency, which was established in order to collect data and make objective decisions, and to function as a creator of environmental knowledge or discourses and as a campaigning organisation. Other European examples are the Group of Policy Advisers and the Joint Research Centre, both of which were created under the auspices of the European Commission, and the European Monitoring Centre on Racism and Xenophobia.

In relation to this, some people speak of knowledge politics. Today's researcher faces numerous investigations, concepts, problems, solutions, theories, descriptions and explanations, embedded in the spirit of science, but also with a scientific standing and political, strategic and administrative function that remains obscure. Once again, this calls for research that takes a step back and questions these investigations, concepts, problems, solutions, theories, descriptions and explanations:

- How have they come into being?
- Which strategies and policies have shaped them?

For example...

Are expressions such as 'the complete colleague', 'lifelong learning' or 'dedicated employees' innocent indications? Or are they a sign of a new form of training, which means that as an employee or citizen you are not only required to perform your duty but to invest your whole life, your soul and your involvement in your organisation or in being a 'good' citizen?

Also, it appears that the subdivision of the social sciences into branches of knowledge related to particular functions in society has become increasingly problematic. Economic science applies to economy; jurisprudence applies to the courts; media studies to the mass media, and so on. Today, more than ever, it is evident that the different fields are helping to invalidate each other. Each field has its own discourse and its own concepts, its own limited resonance; each field can only communicate with itself without regard for the other fields. It becomes difficult to identify one's research with one area of research exclusively, knowing that what looks like progress in one field might very well be detrimental to others. For example, the development within the media of the combination of 'hidden cameras' with 'political journalism' may have created a 'new genre', but this development fundamentally disturbs the political process. Methods have been developed to put a price on 'care' and 'unhealthy lifestyles', but this produces totally unpredictable events within other fields – both positive and negative – possibly without anyone realising it and consequently without the possibility for self-correction. Once again, it therefore seems obvious that we need to take a step back and to question the evolution of the different fields, their communicative closure on their own functions, the limited reflective ability of the individual fields, and their attachment with and detachment from other fields.

Thus, we see the outlines of a new form of questioning appear, which does not merely question actions within a field but which also questions the way questions are asked in the field; questions the emergence of the categories, the problems, the arguments, the themes and the interests. This form of questioning entails a theoretical shift from the primacy of ontology to the primacy of epistemology (Pedersen, 1983), from first-order observations of 'what is out there' to second-order observations of the point that we are watching from when we observe 'what is out there'. From being to becoming.

Ontology and epistemology

Every scientific position entails ontology and epistemology. They point to fundamental questions in every science. Ontology is concerned with the question of basic assumptions about the world and the being of the world; epistemology is concerned with the question of basic assumptions about the precondition of cognition of the world. But not only are there different answers to the two questions; there are also different tensions and hierarchies between them. It makes a fundamental difference whether one begins by answering the question of ontology or by answering the question of epistemology.

An *ontologically over-determined* theory is one that starts with the question of being and asks:

• What does it mean that something exists?
• What are the fundamental possibilities for deciding whether the statement of the theory is true, objective, or scientific?

It is characteristic of ontologically founded thinking that it moves rather swiftly away from these more fundamental questions to the question of method (Habermas, 1972, pp 71-91). The principal methodological question is:

- Which procedures and rules are necessary in order to obtain theoretical knowledge?

For example...

When a survey of the public administration is conducted by sending questionnaires to all leaders of institutions, the method determines the ontology of the administration as establishments represented solely by their leaders. One could say that the method's priority within an ontologically founded thinking nullifies the question of the essential nature of the administration. By its choice of method, it suspends inquiries about the construction of the administration as a particular social phenomenon, the specific characteristics of the administration, the administration's dependency on history, and its function and particulars in relation to other systems. It generally suspends inquiries about the unity of the administration. In conclusion, an ontologically founded thinking produces a presupposition of the object. What you see is taken for granted. It ontologises the administration by reducing it to a certain form of reality that is unquestionable.

Within ontologically over-determined science, methodology holds ultimate priority. The method decides "what exists, or what reality is" (Pedersen, 1983, p 35).

Epistemologically over-determined thinking, on the other hand, is in its nature of second order. It does not primarily ask what but how. It asks:

- In which forms and under which conditions has a certain system of meaning (such as a discourse, a semantics or a system of communication) come into being?
- What are the obstacles to understanding the possibilities of thinking within – but also critically in relation to – an already established system of meaning?
- How and by which analytical strategies can we obtain knowledge critically different from the already established system of meaning? (Pedersen, 1983)

Whereas ontologically over-determined thinking ontologises the object, epistemology *de-ontologises* its object.

Of course, one cannot simply escape ontology by beginning in epistemology and posing the question as one of historical and social conditions of cognition. Every epistemology entails ontology, even in the 'French' version of this theory. But, when you give priority to epistemology, you can work with an *empty* ontology. Empty ontology does not mean that you do not have ontology; rather, it gives an ontological subscription of emptiness to being. It is an ontology that is restricted in its approach to reality, to only saying 'reality is'. The object, however, is not presupposed. In this way, epistemology is concerned with the observation of how the world comes into being as a direct result of the specific perspectives held by individuals, organisations, or systems. It also asks how this causes the world – in the broadest sense – to emerge in specific ways (while the observers themselves also emerge as individuals or organisations). Therefore, an epistemological starting point poses not a question of method, but a question of analytical strategies.

Analytical strategy

Analytical strategy does not consist of methodological rules but rather of a strategy that addresses how the epistemologist will construct the observations of others – organisations or systems – to be the object of his own observations in order to describe the space from which he describes. From an epistemological point of view the perspective constructs both the observer and the observed. Hence analytical *strategy* as a way to stress the deliberate *choice* and its implications, and to highlight that this choice could be made differently with different implications in respect of the emerging object. The problem of the epistemological restriction to '*how*' questions and not 'what' or 'why' questions, is that it constructs the researcher as a 'purist' (that is, as one who does not assume anything in advance about the object to be studied). However, one needs to assume *something* in order to recognise and observe the object. This is the basic condition of working with analytical strategies.

Simply put, the difference between method and analytical strategy can be viewed as follows:

Table 0.1: Method versus analytical strategy[1]

Method	Analytical strategy
Observation of an object	Observation of observations as observations
The goal is to produce true knowledge about a given object	The goal is to question presuppositions, to de-ontologise
What rules and procedures are needed to produce scientific knowledge?	Which analytical strategies will enable us to obtain knowledge, critically different from the existing system of meaning?

This shift from method to analytical strategy raises a number of questions that still have not been answered, and possibly not even conceived of in a satisfactory manner. Within analytical strategy, the question of scientific knowledge poses itself in a different way. Other questions appear and become essential, while certain methodological questions become irrelevant. It is a problem that many constructivist studies do not realise this. The stringent methodological question often fades or disappears because it is not compatible with second-order observations, but far too often it is not superseded by analytical-strategic self-discipline. Instead of method, we often see a pragmatic examination of procedures; the result is often sloppy and inept. Many constructivist studies lack scientific meticulousness in the shape of thorough accounts of their analytical strategies. Often, it is extremely difficult to identify the basis of scientific studies and, unfortunately more often than not, the criticism raised by more mainstream–positivist positions is well justified.

Let me provide just two examples of analytical-strategic difficulties raised by the epistemological turn.

The first example looks at analyses directed at the construction of social identities, such as the construction of an administration, a social movement or a new discourse. Here, the analytical-strategic question of when something can be seen as constructed promptly suggests itself. This is not a methodological problem – it cannot be solved using methodological standards. It is an analytical-strategic problem of establishing the lens through which the evolution of a social movement can be seen.

Without an accurate identification of the conditions necessary for a social movement to be seen as a social movement (and not just as a group or an organisation trying to present itself as a movement), it is virtually impossible to study the construction of a specific social movement and equally impossible to criticise the study of its construction. The more exact the identification, the more sensitive to the empirical is the analysis. Unfortunately, it is not simply a question of choosing a definition, because 'social movements', both in the shape of a social system and as a concept, have an historical evolution of their own to which an analytical strategy must be sensitive.

The other example looks at studies of change. A methodological approach to change would generally be interested in explaining changes – organisational changes, political reforms and so on. In the search for explanations and in the formulation of methods able to examine what causes change, change is typically ontologised. The way change occurs is a given. Whether or not change is seen at all or, if so, in what respect, is ignored.

Studies of change within epistemology, on the other hand, formulate the question of when change can be considered a change. From an epistemological perspective one immediately stumbles across the analytical-strategic difficulty that any formulation of change is based on the observer's construction. Change can only be characterised within the framework of specific differences: a change must have a beginning and an end. Prior to a beginning one must assume an end – whether or not the end provides actual closure. Thus, the nature of any formulation of change is teleological, and the analytical strategy of the epistemological observer must reflect this fact through inquiries and analytical-strategic decisions about the position from which one describes change and, consequently, the distinctions that determine what appears as change to the observer.

The problem holds different definitions in various epistemological programmes. Some are concerned with defining the conditions of an epistemological breakdown, that is, the criteria for defining that point when the observed system of meaning is no longer the same but new (see for example, Regnault, 1983). Luhmann's evolutionary theory focuses on, for one thing, the moment when one principle of differentiation for the construction of new systems of communication is superseded by another (Luhmann, 1990a). In Laclau's discourse analysis, the focus is on the moment when a new nodal point takes over the function of fixating the decentralised elements in the discourse.

About the book

The aim of this book is to contribute to the development of an analytical-strategic language. I attempt to do so by introducing four constructivists with a communication angle – I present them here as analytical strategists and ask the following questions:

- What characterises the way they ask?
- How do their epistemological programmes apply to the observation of observations, the description of descriptions, the signifying of signs?
- How does each of them construct their eye to second-order observations?

This book also juxtaposes four different theories about society as communication or discourse in regard to their analytical strategies. The four theories are Michel Foucault's discourse analysis, Reinhart Koselleck's concept analysis, Ernesto Laclau's discourse theory and Niklas Luhmann's systems theory.

This book is not a broad introduction to the four writers. Rather, it presupposes a certain familiarity with or interest in some form of discourse analysis. Neither does the book aim to weigh the writers' powers of explanation against each other, or to provide some kind of theoretical synthesis. Rather, it attempts to to invoke an analytical-strategic discussion of different ways of defining society as communication. It also aims to see what possibilities for observation unfold when the concern is no longer given objects but, instead, the question of how problems, individuals, interests – all kinds of social identities – come into existence as and within communication. Which analytical difficulties do we encounter when the innocence of the empirical collapses – when we can no longer pretend that 'the object out there' discloses how it wants to be observed, when we know that it is our 'eye' that makes the object appear in a particular way?

Once again, I wish to stress the fact that this book is a *contribution* to the development of an analytical-strategic discourse. I am not certain that my way of presenting the problem is the ultimate one – my argument that the analytical-strategic problem is different from the methodological problem might be incorrect. I do not wish to give the answers to all possible analytical-strategic problems. Neither do I wish to present a manual for discourse analysts.

Rather, I wish to create an outline for the conception and discussion of analytical-strategic problems and, in that respect, the book ought to pose more questions than answers.

The four writers

In this book, I have chosen four ways of seeing – the discourse-analytical, the concept-historical, the discourse-theoretical and the systems-theoretical – because, within my approach, they generate four very different epistemological programmes for second-order observation. Foucault is discourse about discourse, Koselleck conception of concepts, Laclau significations of signifiers and Luhmann observation of observations. The differences between them are used to show the abundance of possible analytical strategies and the abundance of ways in which analytical-strategic problems can be conceived. Traditionally, one is either a systems theorist or discourse analyst. In my approach, the four perspectives fundamentally agree about the emphasis on a new epistemology. The disagreements are over *how*.

Despite their differences, all four share the following notions:

1. Their theories are all programmes for second-order observations.
2. All four theoretical programs are anti-essentialist. Reality contains no essence that requires observation and examination of any specific order. They all presuppose an empty ontology without ascribing anything definitive to reality.
3. They all reject philosophy of consciousness, each in their own way. Luhmann does so by defining society as communication in which different forms of consciousness cannot communicate with each other, but can only exist as the surroundings for communication. Foucault, by a de-centring of the subject into numerous discursive subject positions. Koselleck, by presupposing the forming of ideas to the forming of subjects. Finally, Laclau, by locating the subject in the gap between the uncompleted structure and undecidability.
4. They all reject an ontology of action, that is, the notion that at least actions are real and therefore able to serve as an objective point of reference for examinations within the social sciences. On the contrary, actions are seen as discursive, semantic, or communicative attributes. Actions can be attributed to subjects or systems, or they can attribute them to themselves in the process of constructing a responsible or liable self.
5. Finally, they all settle with the notion of criticism. None of them employs a distinction between uncritical positivism or mainstream thinking on the one hand and themselves as critical on the other. Rather, they are critical of any thinking that claims to be critical! None of them believes that there is a place, an argumentative platform, from which one can be critical in any universal sense. Even so, the rejection of the idea of criticism, and particularly critical theory, plays itself out differently in the four studies.

To elaborate the final point, Luhmann's criticism of critical theory is first and foremost a critique of the notion that there could be a place from which the critic can describe society as a whole. According to Luhmann, there are only systems-relative descriptions of society, and these can never be absolute. Furthermore, Luhmann denounces critical theory for focusing more on how the world is *not* (that is, how the world disappoints the norms of the critic), than on how the world *is* (Luhmann, 1991). Instead, Luhmann's ideal is the unsentimental gaze. Laclau rejects the notion of criticism through a deconstruction of the figure of emancipation as the domicile of the critic, that is, the notion of freedom without power (Laclau, 1996a). Koselleck rejects the notion of criticism through a conceptual-historical analysis of the concept of criticism (Koselleck, 1988). He examines the conditions of its origin and its decline as hypocrisy. Finally, Foucault insists that any truth is always founded on an injustice, which also pertains to his own discursive analyses. Foucault's alternative to the critical researcher is:

> an intellectual, who dissolves self-evident truths and universal explanations, someone who, in the midst of the inertness and restraint of the present, detects and points out the weak points, the openings and the fields of force, someone who is constantly moving and who is not too precisely aware of where he will find himself or what he will be thinking a little into the future, since he is much too preoccupied with the present.... (Schmidt and Kristensen, 1985, p 130)

This book contains four chapters about Foucault's discourse analysis, Koselleck's history of ideas, Laclau's discourse theory and Luhmann's systems theory respectively. The four chapters inquire about the enquiry of these four epistemologists:

- By which fundamental distinctions is the analytical eye shaped?
- How do they create their object?
- Which analytical strategies do they infer?

The output of each of the four epistemologists is very different. Some have produced reasonably few, but concentrated, theoretical studies, others have primarily conducted concrete analyses and their analytical-strategic contributions stem from these works, others have an output that is vast in size, theoretically as well as analytically. Although I ask the same questions in regard to the different epistemologists, the approach is necessarily different with each one, hence the different representations of the four epistemologists both in size and style. The benefit of this is that it consolidates the width of the analytical-strategic problems that emerge. In the concluding chapter I offer a more explicit formulation of what I mean by analytical strategy. Moreover, in the conclusion I conduct a more direct comparison of the four analytical strategies, although knowing that this is an impossible venture, I attempt to line them up and let them reflect each other.

Delimiting marks

It is obvious to ask, why not four other writers? Why not include, for example, Habermas, Bourdieu and Fairclough? It could be argued that Jürgen Habermas really ought to be considered in a book that is founded on the notion of society as communication, as, since the 1960s, Habermas has observed the linguistic turn of the social sciences. In my view, however, Habermas represents a transitional figure between ideological criticism and discourse analysis. He sees the unavoidable centrality of language and communication, but he does not fully live out the consequences.

As early as 1965, in his book *Knowledge and human interests* (Habermas, 1972), Habermas realises that it is necessary to settle with ideological criticism and the distinction it creates between true and false consciousness. However, he refuses to give up the universal status of the concept of criticism; rather, he aimed to find a new way to base criticism. His first proposal for this can be found in an article about universal pragmatism (that is, dialogue without hegemony directed at understanding) (Habermas, 1991). Later, he displaces and reformulates his universalistic concept of criticism several times, for example in his ethics of discourse (Habermas, 1992) and, most recently, in the weighty tome *Between facts and norms* (Habermas, 1996). But, the fact remains that he never establishes a programme for second-order observation, which simultaneously admits to its status as first-order observation. His insistence on a universalistic foundation implies that, when observing communication through his theoretical programme, it is always by means of an ideal about communication. This means that Habermas cannot observe observations as observations but always has to observe them as deviations from a universal regularity. Habermas has committed himself to observing the way the world is not rather than the way it is. Thus, Habermas's programme remains in the quagmire of ideological criticism, even if it is a very advanced version.

I could also have included Pierre Bourdieu in this book and, indeed, contemplated it for a long time. Many of Bourdieu's works contain reflections of analytical strategy. In my own empirical discourse analysis I have, on several occasions, employed elements from Bourdieu's analytics. When comparing Bourdieu and Habermas, they very often read the same texts but from completely different perspectives. They both read the works of Searl and Austin, for example, about different types of speech actions. But while Habermas inquires about the universal conditions of speech actions directed at understanding, Bourdieu inquires about the historical institutional conditions that authorise a specific person as the generator of specific speech actions (Bourdieu, 1992). It is my understanding that Bourdieu pursues a double strategy. On one hand, he is without doubt an epistemologist and thinks, therefore, in terms of analytical strategy – he always inquires about the origins of problems, fields and speech actions. On the other hand, he appears to have trouble accepting the cool gaze of epistemology and often resorts, therefore, to metaphysics of suppression as if the distinction between over and under were universally designed. He seems to be in constant oscillation between a first- and second-order programme for observation; between letting go of ideological criticism and falling back on it.

Finally, it is pertinent to ask, why not Norman Fairclough? I believe that the wide base that discourse analysis gained in the 1990s is largely the achievement of Norman Fairclough (see for example, Fairclough, 1995). In particular, he has made discourse analysis accessible to linguistically inclined researchers, but also to certain parts of the social sciences. One of his achievements is the linking of discourse analysis with text analysis (Fairclough, 1992), and with his tight empirical analysis he has lifted discourse analysis out of a postmodern theoretical fetishism. In many ways, his ambitions are close to those of this book. I do believe, however, that he remains within a relatively more classical methodological thinking, with the result that the epistemological objective in discourse analysis does not appear clearly in his writings. I find it hard, in other words, to recognise the unique discourse-analytical eye in Fairclough. This does not mean that I fail to appreciate his many competent analyses – it might also just point to my own narrow concept of analytical strategy (see Chouliaraki and Fairclough, 1999).

My own path to the analytical-strategic question

Let me give a brief, and I hope helpful, account of my own relationship with analytical strategy. This book has not come into being purely as a result of theoretical deskwork (although that has also been necessary). I have not invented the analytical-strategic question out of the blue; it has presented itself to me in a number of concrete empirical studies in which I have applied some kind of epistemological analysis. As time has gone by, I have simply needed to formulate a more concise definition of the analytical-strategic question. And there is more to come.

My own work has always played itself out in the space between theory and empirical studies. It has focused on analysing how different ideas have shaped the world, and the analytical-strategic problem of observing these ideas without becoming a slave to them and without simply reducing them and judging them from the perspective of a different idea has always presented itself.

In the book *Selvskabt Forvaltning (The autopoiesis of the administration)* (Andersen, 1995), I asked two questions:

1. How is a certain political and administrative discourse invented and propagated?
2. And what is the effect of the propagation of this discourse on the constituent character of the administration?

The first question was initiated by the rapid modernisation of the public sector and by the fact that administrative policies appeared to establish a new discursive regime. I wanted to describe this regime and its shaping, but I was not interested in criticising it from a normative position, such as, for instance, 'the defence of the welfare state'. The first question addresses how something is constructed; hence, the analytical-strategic question asks how it is at all possible to study a discourse under construction. In order to be able to study the construction or the origin of something, one has to be able to modify the origin and ascribe unambiguous criteria to the moment when one states that something has come into being. Here, I adopted and maintained Pedersen's distinction between ideal, discourse and institution. The analytical-strategic problem primarily consisted of defining clear and observable measures for when something was an ideal, when this ideal could be said to have developed into a discourse and, finally, when this discourse could be said to have become institutionalised.

The second question about the constituent effects on the administration was initiated by the distinctive characteristics of administrative policies. First, they are policies of the second order: they are policies about the administrative framework for politics. Second, they are policies that cover the boundaries of the administration, including the relationships between public and private, administration and citizen, administration and employee, and also between administration and politics. Administrative policies appear not only to alter conditions within the public sector, but also to change the entire conception of what can be understood as the public sector.

Consequently, the second question addressed systemic disruptions, and so the analytical-strategic question became: How it is possible to locate systemic disruptions as such? The dilemma presents itself as a question of when a given system – here the public administration – is no longer the same system but a new one. To understand this further, I used Luhmann's systems theory and defined the problem as a question of how displacements happen within the internal differentiation forms of the administrative system. Any administration contains numerous sub-systems; the differentiation form is the conformity in the sub-system's way of being different from each other and from each of their respective surroundings. If I could demonstrate that the differentiation form was no longer the same, I would have shown that the administration was no longer the same. That is to say that a displacement of the administration's internal differentiation form means that sub-administrations are no longer formed and developed in the same way – that their constitution is radically different.

My work with these two questions led me within my dissertation on the development of administrative politics and the administration in 20th-century Denmark), to the formulation of a particular analytical strategy which I have named *institutional history* (Andersen, 1994). One of the focal points of my dissertation was to show how the boundaries of the administration were put at stake and changed through administrative policies. This opened up new theoretical questions about how the connections between systems are changed when their boundaries are threatened. Until this point I have dealt with the boundary between public/private and politics/administration.

In reference to the public/private boundary, I raised the question about the constitution of the private sector in relation to the redefinition of boundaries on the part of the public sector (Andersen, 1996). My thesis was that outsourcing does not simply lead to more market and less politics, but that private corporations that orient themselves towards public markets are forced to subscribe to the discursive codes of the political system, that is, they are forced to constitute themselves anew. Thus, the boundary between politics and economy is no longer more or less identical to the difference between public organisations and private corporations. Within public markets the boundary between politics and economy penetrates the internal communication of private corporations. Here, the question focuses on the relationship between organisation and function system and on how private organisations can associate themselves with different function systems, including the political and the economic systems. The analytical-strategic question is concerned with how to study the emergence of a private corporation whose identity is not necessarily consistent but is relative to the association with either the political code or the economic code. This required the formulation of an entirely new analytical strategy in regard to institutional history – an analytical strategy capable of pertaining to the organisational level, separating organisational communication from other forms of communication.

In a book analysing the history of the outsourcing debate (Andersen, 1997), again, I required a new analytical strategy. Unlike the study of the origin of administrative politics, there is no single discourse on outsourcing. Rather than being an autonomous discourse, outsourcing is and has been a drifting concept whose meaning is interjected simultaneously in numerous mutually conflicting discourses. Hence the predicament was not (as in the question of administrative politics) the examination of the construction and institutionalisation of one discourse, but rather the unfolding of interdiscursive relationships within time and space surrounding the concept of outsourcing. The analytical-strategic task involved defining the criteria for when and how a relationship exists, which also means when and how a discursive separation exists. For this purpose, I developed a genealogical analytical strategy based on the works of Michel Foucault.

My latest book, *Kærlighed og omstilling – italesættelsen af den offentligt ansatte* (*Love and reorganisation – the articulation of the public employee*), makes inquiries into the boundary between public administration and employee (Andersen and Born, 2001). The book examines the articulation of 'the employee' over the past 150 years in Denmark. In the past, the relationship between employee and organisation was discussed in an impersonal fashion, in which duties and rights were the focus. Today, however, the employee is also required to 'love' the employing organisation and to share its outlook, otherwise he or she ought to leave before being racked by feelings of guilt. In the language of employment policies, this is termed 'involvement', 'initiative' and the 'responsible employee'. The analytical strategy used in this book is inspired by the work of Luhmann and Koselleck, with a Foucauldian slant. The book combines three analytical strategies: a semantic historical-analytical strategy, a differentiation analysis and a form/medium analysis of the coding of employee communication. The semantic analysis examines the conceptual history of the employee – we look at how the employee is created in different semantic regimes. The differentiation analysis relates the semantic development to the development in the 'unity of the administration' over 100 years during which the public institution changes from the 'innocent institution' via the 'professionally responsible institution' into the 'strategic organisation'. In the strategic organisation, the codes of the conversation become fleeting. Subsequently, the form/medium analysis pertains to the *codes* that become available to the communication about the relationship between employee and organisation. The focus is on three codes: the legal code (right/wrong), the educational code (better/worse learning competencies) and the code of love (loved/not loved). The code chosen for the specific communication determines who can communicate about what, including what can be considered as a good argument. Finally, the focus shifts to the way in which inclusion and exclusion takes place. With love's codification of the communication it becomes the responsibility of the employee to be included in the workplace. Exclusion becomes self-exclusion.

In the encounter with empirical studies, I have, over time, been able to locate different analytical-strategic problems. I have defined various analytical strategies pertaining to certain epistemological research questions. But one of the difficulties I have encountered, which this book addresses, is the lack of a general, well-defined concept of analytical strategy capable of describing what an analytical strategy consists of. I have always been of the opinion that there is not, and cannot, be one analytical strategy capable of answering all the questions that a creative epistemologist could possibly ask. I have always encouraged students and others to define their own analytical strategy in respect to their field of interest and their questions. In many ways, this seems like an unfair request when one is not able to clearly explicate what an analytical strategy is or when an analytical strategy is a good strategy; when there is not even a single book or article that addresses the question in detail.

Since there is not one true analytical strategy, it makes no sense to grant priority to any theoretical trend (for example that of Foucault or Luhmann). I have always skipped between different epistemological schools and have been happy to combine elements if they fit the specific analytical strategy. Hence, this book should be regarded as an attempt to speak of analytical strategy in general terms, and to create a field that enables analytical-strategic discussions across the boundaries of different epistemological trends. The book may make difficult reading to some people; the ambition, nevertheless, is not theory for the sake of theory but rather the improvement of empirical analyses within the epistemological realm. What is the purpose of professing to discourse analysis if one does not conduct actual, empirically founded discourse analyses?

Note

[1] The distinction should not be understood as a normative regulation against the use of methods for discourse analysts. The central question is whether a methodological or a discourse-analytical perspective is primary in the research design. Naturally, within one analytical strategy different methods can be introduced which the analytical strategy must then question.

The discourse analysis of Michel Foucault

More than anyone, Michel Foucault has developed and created an agenda for discourse analysis. Moreover, he has received the widest recognition within the social sciences. At present, he functions as nothing short of a guru within research on economic regulation, and has inspired, for example, analyses of the genealogy of financial management and calculation.

Although I have studied Foucault longer than any other writer, he is probably still the one I have the most difficulty in presenting. There are several reasons for this.

First, for the more subjective reason that, having dealt with a particular work over a long period of time, it is difficult to maintain a distance from it; gradually you invent your own Foucault that might be more telling of yourself than of Foucault. If anyone feels that my readings abuse Foucault, this could be why.

Second, Foucault has fundamentally failed in one respect. He has founded a school of thought even though it was his explicit ambition not to do so. Today, there are researchers of Foucault in the same way that there are researchers of Kierkegaard or Benjamin. His works have turned into philosophical monuments. A vast number of books have been written about him: Foucault the philosopher, the person, the historian, the political theorist, the aesthetic, the ethicist, the sociologist, and, in this case, the analytical strategist. As with Marx in the 1970s, it is now almost impossible to refer to Foucault without being held accountable for various readings of Foucault. The worst thing to do is to allude to Dreifuss and Rabinow; then, one is characterised as an 'Anglo-Saxon' (which is not a distinguished trait). In what follows, Foucault will be read as a discourse analyst, which he was, although not exclusively. Generally, Foucault can be defined as a formation analyst, who, for certain periods, ascribed a principal position to discourse analysis, yet, at other times, granted it a more secondary position in relation to, for example, institutional analysis.

Third, Foucault's particular way of creating concepts makes it difficult to present them without depleting them in relation to his own definitions. All concepts are created through distinctions. In the work of Laclau and Luhmann, all concepts are bivalent, meaning that they possess two sides – this makes them more easy to manage. Foucault's concepts, on the other hand, are polyvalent – they are many-sided and often come into being through countless negative delimitations and very few, if any, positive definitions. In a presentation such as this, it is very difficult not to reduce Foucault's valencies.

Fourth, Foucault's work is rather unsystematic. It is not possible, therefore, to draw out a coherent discourse theory from his work. Again, this is related to the fact that he did not want to create a school of thought. In the words of Lars Henrik Schmidt: "His analytics is simply too consciously unsystematic for it to develop into an actual *theory*; he himself does not even cohere to the more programmatic proposals which nevertheless exist. It is primarily a particular analytics, a practice which beckons meditation and imitation without possible repetition" (Schmidt and Kristensen, 1985, p 5).

Rather than theory, the outcome of Foucault's works consists of a number of analytical strategies and analytical-strategic examinations of, for example, periodisations, delimitation of discourses, monuments rather than documents and demonstrations of rupture. This is where Foucault's strength lies, but these analytical strategies are always defined in relation to a specific research question, a specific problem, and hence the question is whether they thereby allow for simple generalisation. That, however, is precisely my goal.

Foucault as a structuralist

Foucault is often called structuralist or poststructuralist. That makes sense given the fact that he developed his discourse analysis in an environment of structuralists, especially his teacher, the Marxist and ideology theorist Louis Althusser. However, he has, on several occasions, rejected both those labels. In this book Foucault will be read as a phenomenologist, without consciousness as the origin of meaning – a subjectless phenomenology.

Structuralists work from a distinction between the manifest surface and the latent structure. Structuralist analysis reconstructs the hidden and latent structure based on logical breaches on the manifest level. In other words, structuralists work from the idea that, underneath the visible, directly accessible text, lays a slightly displaced invisible text that controls the questions and answers posed by the visible text. The invisible text amounts to a regime that condemns specific questions. By directing attention toward those moments in the manifest text when meaning breaks down – when answers are given without questions and when questions are posed without answers – structuralism can raise questions regarding the underlying text, which must exist so that the apparently illogical and meaningless makes sense after all. In Althusser, it is called symptomatic reading, that is, a reading of the logical breaches of the visible text as symptoms of an underlying and controlling structure (Althusser and Balibar, 1970). Poststructuralists maintain the notion of structure but see the structure as much more loose and undecided. Foucault rejects both positions. To Foucault there is only one level, which is that of appearance. Foucault focuses on the statements as they emerge, as they come into being. It is crucial to him never to reduce them to something else. Consequently, discourse is not a structure to Foucault; a point to which we will return later in this chapter.

However, if we were nevertheless to associate Foucault with structuralism (which does in some respects seems fair, since his entire position is developed within a structuralist environment), he could be called a *transformation structuralist*. First, he would not define the notion of structure within a synchronous perspective as, for example, in the works of de Saussure, Lévi-Strauss and Althusser. Structure would then be transferred into a diachronic analytics, precisely as a transformational structure, asserting itself at moments of change and rupture. Hence, structures would not be an attribute of the world but of the diachronic story. Consequently, transformational structures are not structures that are uncovered, but rather the writer's construction of the historical relationship between discourse and institution.

Foucault as a discourse analyst

Foucault's fundamental concern is the questioning of discursive assumptions. He challenges individual will and reason by showing how every utterance is an utterance within a specific discourse to which certain rules of acceptability apply. Foucault challenges knowledge as a neutral speech position by showing that humanities and the social sciences in particular are inseparable from moralising projects; that humanities and the social sciences do not simply elucidate the world but establish regimes of knowledge and truth that regulate our approach to ourselves, each other and our surroundings respectively. Foucault wants to show how any discourse involves excluding procedures, which not only exclude themes, arguments and speech positions from the discourse, but also produce outsiders, denounce groups of people as sick, abnormal or irrational, and grant other groups the right and legitimacy to treat these people (for example by imprisonment or therapy). Foucault wants to show how power in society cannot be pinpointed, and thus separated and isolated from, for example, the social sciences and public welfare institutions such as schools and hospitals, and that power is ubiquitous as a productive factor. Power is present in our approach to things insofar as the objects we relate to are always discursive objects, produced by and in discourse. Power is present in our approach to ourselves insofar as our self-relation is a product of power. Power is present in our approach to others insofar as, for example, 'criminals', 'mad people' or 'sick people' are not in and of themselves criminal, mad or sick. Conversely, criminality and illness are discursive positions, which are established with the intent to control.

Madness and mental illness

In *Madness and civilization*, Foucault (1971) seeks to examine the emergence of the empty negativity of modern reason – folly. His thesis is that madness participates in producing reason by being the other side of reason. There can be no reason without reason recognising itself as such. That requires reason to be able to exclude and separate itself from folly. The genealogy of madness is thus not a story of the conquests of psychology and psychiatry; it is not a study of the language of reason but of the silence of folly and madness (Foucault, 1971). To a certain extent, it is a study of the conditions of the origins of modern discoursivity, that is, of that which fundamentally defines discourse as discourse within modernity. Guided by the discursive boundary between reason and madness, Foucault examines the constituent relations between reason and madness. He examines the excluding procedures and forms of reason, and hence of society, including inclusive forms of exclusion.

Illness is one example of an inclusive form of exclusion. Illness is a position in society: by defining 'madness' as illness, that which is excluded from society can be kept under control within society.

The discursive history of the reason/madness boundary can be roughly divided into four periods. In the Middle Ages, 'mad people' were looked on as a kind of ideal, from whom one could learn something. Mad people were believed to possess a more immediate relationship with God; they were closer to God than other people. In the Christian search for salvation, mad people therefore possessed something generally desirable. In the second period (the 17th-18th centuries), the perception of mad people changed from one of consecration to one of 'sickness'. Mad people were feared and locked up together with the poor and the criminal, not in order to help and treat them but in order to 'dispose' of them. Mad people were thought to set a bad example in the face of the new work ethic, in which it was believed that idleness was the root of all evil. Mad people represented idleness and lacked the ability to actively partake in production. They were therefore a disgrace. The third period (the 19th century) defined differences between madness, criminality and poverty. Mad people were locked up in hospitals, where attempts were made to 'cure' them (in this context, curing means reinstalling in the mad person a sense of dependency, humility and gratitude towards society). One of the methods used in this treatment was cold showers and baths, which were meant to revive the spirits of the mad person; another was to inject new blood into the veins of the patient in order to boost the blood circulation. There were no distinctions made between the psychological and the physical. Not until the fourth period (the 20th-21st centuries) does such a distinction occur. Now, we attempt to understand mental illness and to perceive 'madness' based on 'mad people's' experiences and their distortion of reality. We now aim to restore communication – not only between the mad and the sane person, but also between the mad and sane aspects of the adapted personality.

As a study of the transformational conditions of modern discoursivity, *Madness and civilization* is, furthermore, a study of that which modern society recognises as its history. In the words of Vincent Descombes:

> Foucault intends to sound the limits of what we can recognize as *our* history. At the interior of this history of ours, as of all history, identity presides; within it, a single culture enables a number of human beings to articulate a collective 'we'. This identity – here is what must now be demonstrated – is constituted through a series of exclusions. [...] Foucault goes further and asserts that the history of madness is the history of the possibility of history. 'History', as we understand it, implies in effect the accomplishment of works

and the transmission of words endowed with meaning. Now madness, according to Foucault, is defined by 'the absence of works'. The mad person's gestures culminate in nothing, his delirious talk refers to nothing: his life is fundamentally workless and inoperative. The possibility of history rests upon the decision that all gestures and words which afford no positive significance be rejected as unreason. Madness surrounds history on all sides: it is there *before* history and is still there *after* history. (Descombes, 1980)

In *Mental illness and psychology*, Foucault (1976) examines the conditions within psychology of speaking of illness. How is the notion of illness construed? Where does psychology find its concepts of illness? And how do these concepts of illness place psychology in a particular relationship with the patient? Foucault defines four questions:

1. Under what conditions can one speak of illness in the psychological domain?
2. What relations can one define between the facts of mental pathology and those of organic pathology?
3. How did our culture come to give mental illness the meaning of deviancy and, to the patient, a status that excludes him?
4. And how, despite that fact, does our society express itself in those morbid forms in which it refuses to recognise itself? (Foucault, 1976)

The first two questions address the way in which the question of illness operates *within* the pathological discourse. Foucault explores the shaping of the psyche through the creation of various forms of analysis in psychology, primarily historical and phenomenological analysis. He observes the way psychology and psychoanalysis observe their patients. He observes, for example, how mental illnesses occur when psychoanalysis views its patients through the concept of the individual story. He thus inquires about the discursive figures that cause particular individual behaviour to emerge as illness. By answering the first two questions, Foucault has presented the *forms* of appearance of illness, but not yet the *conditions* of its appearance. He seeks to uncover the latter through the last two questions, which address the construction of madness outside psychology. Once again, the boundary between reason and folly becomes central to the analysis. Foucault's thesis is that those psychological analyses that define the ill person as an outsider are projections of specific cultural and discursive themes. Foucault shows how man has become "a 'psychologizable species' only when his relation to madness made a psychology possible, that is to say, when his relation to madness was defined by the external dimensions of exclusion and punishment and by the internal dimensions of moral assignment and guilt" (Foucault, 1976, p 73). Foucault concludes:

Psychology can never tell the truth about madness because it is madness that holds the truth of psychology. [...] There is a very good reason why psychology can never master madness; it is because psychology became possible in our world only when madness had already been mastered and excluded from the drama. (Foucault, 1976, pp 74, 87)

History and humanity

In *The order of things*, Foucault (1974) shifts the focus onto his own scientific discourse and its historical conditions. He sets out to examine the historical conditions of structuralism[1]. He raises the question of why structuralism becomes a dominant societal phenomenon, manifesting itself in a large number of humanist sciences: in structuralist psychoanalysis with Lacan as the main figure (for example, Lacan, 2001), in structuralist ethnology and anthropology with Lévi-Strauss (for example, Lévi-Strauss, 1996) and in a structuralist literary criticism with writers like Barthes and Kristeva (Kristeva, 1989; Barthes, 1990). In all three cases, Foucault particularly subscribes to structuralist linguistics with Fernando de Saussure as the primary point of reference (de Saussure, 1990). Foucault investigates how language replaces man as the object of knowledge. Foucault simultaneously studies the origin and disappearance of the humanities as a result of the repression of human beings by language. In Classicism, 'man' is considered the centre of the world – man is defined as the subject in an double extension of, on one hand, a transcendental being charged with will and reason, and, on the other hand, an empirical being (as specific people that can be observed). This defines the potential conditions of the humanities as humans observing humans. However, through structuralism, language becomes subject by a similar division into both a transcendent and an empirical being. It is no longer humans but structures that speak – 'it' speaks as Lacan formulates it; the conditions of the humanities recede. Instead, we are faced with language, speaking of itself through itself. Foucault says, "where there is a sign, there man cannot be, and where one makes signs speak, there man must fall silent" (Foucault, 1998a, p 266). In other words, discourse analysis becomes central.

With *The order of things*, Foucault makes structuralism the object of discourse analysis and seeks to distance himself from it by analysing structuralism and its genealogy. He begins in structuralism and writes his way out of it through discourse analysis. In *Discipline and punish*, Foucault (1977) asks:

Where does this strange practice and the peculiar project of locking someone up in order to rediscipline them, which is implied by the criminal law of the modern age, stem from? [...] Behind the insight into people and behind the humanity of the punishments we rediscover a particular disciplinary investment in the human bodies, a mixture of submission and objectification, one and the same relation between 'knowledge–power'. Is it possible to define the genealogy of modern morality based on a political history of the bodies? (Krause-Jensen, 1978, author's translation)

Discipline and punish

Discipline and punish traces the history of prison and describes how the types of surveillance and punishment change fundamentally from the beginning of the 19th century. The change is outlined as a shift from the torment and absolute monarchy of the Middle Ages, to the modern prisons, in which the apprehension of punishment, rather than the appalling theatre of torment and torture, is supposed to deter people from criminal acts. In the modern prison, "the convicted body is no longer displayed, now it is hidden. It is no longer destroyed, but instead detained and isolated because it carries something, which can be tamed and trained" (Krause-Jensen, 1978, p 124, author's translation). This is not a simple movement from barbarism to humanism, but rather a movement defined by the rise of disciplining as a new and effective form of power. An expression of this displacement is Bentham's famous Panopticon – a prison in which prisoners do not know if or when they are being observed; in which the observer cannot himself be observed, forcing the prisoners to discipline themselves based on the notion of constant surveillance: "The Panopticon is a machine for dissociating the see/being seen dyad: in the peripheric ring, one is totally seen, without ever seeing; in the central tower, one sees everything without ever being seen" (Foucault, 1977). The movement is from public torment to hidden surveillance, where the soul, not the body, is to be punished.

However, *Discipline and punish* is not only a book about prisons. It is a book about how a particular power of normalisation – disciplining and surveillance – is shaped in conjunction with the rise of the prison but is later propagated and generalised in society. In Foucault's understanding, the prison is not simply an institution subordinate to the courts of justice. Conversely, prison is a form that subjects itself to the courts and also prevails in a large number of relationships in society at large. Foucault speaks of the relative carceral continuity as the many connections that exist between, on the one hand, the surveillance and disciplining forms and, on the other hand, institutions such as education, social services and workplaces with organised hierarchy:

> The judges of normality are present everywhere. We are in the society of the teacher-judge, the doctor-judge, the educator-judge, the 'social worker'-judge; it is on them that the universal reign of the normative is based; and each individual, wherever he may find himself [sic], subjects to it his body, his gestures, his behaviour, his aptitudes, his achievements. The carceral networks, in its compact or disseminated forms, with its systems of insertion, distribution, surveillance, observation, has been the greatest support, in modern society, of the normalizing power. (Foucault, 1977, p 304)

Foucault's analytical strategy develops parallel with this shift in his questioning. In this chapter, I make a distinction between four analytical strategies: the archaeology of knowledge, genealogy, self-technology analysis and dispositive analysis. In certain readings of Foucault, the analytical strategies successively replace each other. In my reading, they are constructed on top of one another. My outlines of Foucault's analytical strategies are not complete, however; it is possible to trace other strategies in his work, for example an aesthetic analysis.

Archaeological discourse analysis

The archaeology of knowledge (1986a) is Foucault's first major attempt at describing his efforts, and is a rationalisation and systematisation of his prior works rather than a programme for his future work. Foucault never consistently adhered to his own knowledge-archaeological analytical strategy, so there is no reason for the rest of us to be literal in our reading of it. *The archaeology of knowledge* was never intended to be a methodical description for systematised repetition and imitation; however, it is useful as a catalogue of the analytical-strategic questions that arise in attempts to invoke discourse without taking to structuralism or other forms of reductionism.

The knowledge archaeology installs a distinction between statement, discourse and discursive formation. These three concepts provide a joint foundation for discourse analysis:

- *statement* is the atom of discourse – its smallest unit;
- *discourse* is the final, actually demarcated body of formulated statements – it is the archive of the discourse analyst;
- *discursive formation* is a system of dispersion for statements; it is the regularity in the dispersion of statements.

However, discourse is not a structure and does not exist on a level different from statements. Statements do not manifest themselves as a discursive structure. Discursive formation simply consists of the regularity of the irregular distribution of statements. In other words, the fundamental guiding difference in Foucault's knowledge archaeology is regularity/dispersion of statements. This is the basic difference in Foucault's analyses of discourse:

> Whenever one can describe, between a number of statements, such a system of dispersion, whenever, between objects, types of statements, concepts, or thematic choices, one can define a regularity, we will say, for the sake of convenience, that we are dealing with a discursive formation. (Foucault, 1986a, p 38)

The difference entails an ontological asymmetry. Whereas, according to Foucault, the statements actually exist, regularity is a construction that is created through discourse analysis. Hence, it is the discourse analyst who constructs the regularity of the dispersion, that is the discursive formation. My questions are:

- How is this conducted?
- When is a statement a statement?
- When is regularity a regularity that can be defined as discursive formation?

These are the fundamental analytical-strategic problems. What the discourse analyst is concerned with – that which is, according to Foucault, the object of discourse analysis – is *statements* (*énoncé*). As the building blocks of discourse, the way a statement is demarcated is of the utmost significance for the formation of discourse analysis. Like Foucault, I will first outline what statements are not, that is, what discourse analysis does not analyse.

Discourse analysis is not textual analysis

According to Foucault, a discourse does not consist of texts and discourse analysis is therefore not textual analysis. Texts, as such, are much too boundless for them to function as the basis for discourse analysis. Although books serve a particular purpose and possess certain economic value, they are not independent discursive units:

> The outlines of a book are never clearly and stringently defined: no book can exist by its own powers; it always exists due to its conditioning and conditional relations to other books; it is a point in a network; it carries a system of references – explicitly or not – to other books, other texts, or other sentences; and the structure of reference, and thereby the entire complex system of autonomy and heteronomy, depends on whether we are dealing with a dissertation on physics, a collection of political speeches, or a science fiction novel. It is true that the book presents itself as a tangible object; it clings to the tiny parallelepiped surrounding it: but its unity is variable and relative, does not let itself be constructed or stated and therefore cannot be described outside a discursive field. (Foucault, 1970, p 152, author's translation)

Discourse analysis is not literary analysis

Like texts, the works of authors are not bound wholes: "Apparently it indicates the sum of texts that can be denoted by a proper name" (Foucault, 1970, p 153). However, says Foucault, how about texts that are signed under a pseudonym? How about hasty notes or sketches that are discovered posthumously? What, for example, should be considered as belonging to the works of Nietzsche? Only the books? Or also letters and postcards and texts signed Kaiser Nietzsche? The fundamental problem, however, consists in the general tendency to perceive works, as heterogeneous as they might be, as the embodiment of one writer's thoughts, experiences or unconscious. In other words, to view texts as the indication of a whole, which is not visible in the textual fragments but must be ascribed through interpretation. Consequently,

Foucault delivers a critique not only of actual literary analysis but of any textual analysis, which professes to refer the statements of the text back to the author and his intentions, concerns, unconscious, circumstances and so on.

Discourse analysis is not structural analysis

Statements do not express an unspoken structure that secretly animates every statement. The discourse at hand is, in the end, not simply the disturbing presence of the unspoken (Foucault, 1970, pp 154-5).

Discourse analysis is not a form of discourse commentary

To comment on discourses means to inquire about the statement, meaning and intention of discourses. Discourse commentary attempts to expose the underlying meaning of the stated, based on the assumption that the deeper meaning comes closer to an essential truth. According to Foucault, however, commenting means an admittance of access to the signified over the signifier. His ensuing question is whether it is possible, conversely, to construct a discourse analysis capable of escaping the fate of commentary by presupposing that the stated only exists in its historical rise and emergence (Foucault, 1986b, p 17).

Subsequently discourse analysis becomes an analysis of statements in their *positivity*:

> Every discursive moment (that is, every statement) must be observed in its positive suddenness, in this punctuality which it enters and in this temporal dispersion which makes it possible to repeat it, realise, forget, transform, efface it until the last traces, hide it, far from all eyes, in the dust of books. (Foucault, 1970, p 155, author's translation)

Foucault calls discourse analysis "pure description of discursive facts" (Foucault, 1972, p 234). He even maintains that the spirit of discourse analysis is a felicitous positivism (p 234).

Analysis of statements

In short, a statement needs to be analysed in its appearance, as it emerges, and cannot be reduced to expressing anything other than itself, such as, for example, the intention of the statement, the context, the concern or the meaning of the statement. Foucault rejects any reductive or interpretative statement descriptions. He consistently avoids questions of *what* or *why* in relation to statements but only asks *how*. The question 'What is the meaning of the statement?' instantly ontologises the statement – it is reduced to a given, containing a secret. The question 'Why this statement?' reduces the statement to its cause. Only questions of how the statement appears grant full attention to the statement, only *how* does not immediately shift the attention away from the statement itself to that which could possibly provide the statement with a meaning or an explanation.

- When, then, is a statement a statement?
- How do we recognise a statement?

To Foucault, a statement is a *function of existence* that enables groups of signs to exist (Foucault, 1986a, pp 86-8). What does that mean? It means that *the statement is the smallest unit, which brings forth phenomenon through enunciation.* We are thus able to recognise the statement by its momentary creation rather than by its appearance as a sign, sentence, book or argument. Statements are positive events that produce existence through enunciation. This function of existence contains at least four aspects: object, subject, conceptual network and strategy.

Discursive objects

A statement is only a statement if it creates objects. Those objects referred to by a statement are not 'objects in themselves' or 'objects out there', they are discursive objects constructed, classified and identified by the statement itself. The statement creates the object to which it refers through enunciation. The enunciation of the object implies that it is brought to life as a social and discursive fact and can therefore be articulated (Foucault, 1986a, pp 88-92).

Subjects

A statement can only be regarded as a statement if it creates subject positions that can be signed over to individuals, that is, if the statement creates discursive spaces from which something can be stated. The question is:

- In which positions can, and must, the statement be held by an individual, for the individual to become the subject of the statement?

Again, subjects do not stand outside of the statement; conversely, the statement articulates the space and possibility of subjects.

Conceptual network

A statement can only be regarded as a statement if it situates its elements of signification in a space in which they can breed and multiply. Any statement subscribes to certain concepts, and yet it is not simply a variation of conceptual combinations. The status of the concept is determined by the statement, through the statement's endowment of an associated field that consists of all the formulations that the statement implicitly or explicitly refers to, either by repeating them, modifying them, adapting them, opposing them or commenting on them. According to Foucault, all statements re-actualise other statements in some way. Linguistic elements such as signs and sentences are only statements if they are immersed in an associated field, in which they simultaneously appear as unique elements. Foucault summarises it thus:

> There is no statement in general, no free, neutral, independent statement; but a statement always belongs to a series or a whole, always plays a role among other statements, deriving support from and distinguishing itself from them: it is always part of a network of statements, in which it has a role, however minimal it may be, to play. (Foucault, 1986a, p 99)

This should not only be understood retrospectively as the fact that the statement becomes a statement by relating to prior statements, but also understood progressively as the way in which the statement paves the way for potential future statements. Hence, a statement becomes a statement only if it both re-actualises and extends other statements. This enunciative function, by the way, has a striking resemblance to Luhmann's notion of meaning, which is discussed in Chapter Four.

According to Luhmann, meaning is merely the unity of actualisation and potentialisation. Conversely, the enunciative function differs significantly from Laclau's more poststructuralist theory of signification, which is concerned with structural relations between elements. I propose that perhaps Foucault's discourse analysis and Luhmann's systems theory are closer to one another than Foucault's discourse analysis and Laclau's discourse theory because of their phenomenological kinship.

Strategy

A statement can be defined as a statement only if it is integrated into operations or strategies in which the identity of the statement is maintained or effaced (Foucault, 1986a, pp 100-5). A statement is not simply that which is stated independently of time, place and materiality. A statement always chooses a materiality, at least in the form of a medium for its creation, for example speech, writing, report, arrangement or image. It always seeks support in a context; it appears with a status derived from the strategic context of its origin. It is always strategic in the sense that the statement as re-actualisation emerges as one choice among other possible actualisations. Consequently, it cannot easily be displaced in time and space.

For example...

Regardless of the attempted analogies, the readaptation for the screen of the books of Morten Korck is not an identical transcription of the 'original' statements. The statements are repeated, but their materiality and strategic standing is different. The fact that Lars von Trier is responsible for the screen version is an enunciative event, which exceeds the film itself.

Therefore, discourse analysis consists of an analysis of statements, in which statements exist as an event, constantly enunciating subject positions, discursive objects, conceptual relations and strategies. The world comes into being, so to speak, through the statement as event.

Constructing the archive

Statements are always statements in a *discourse*. The field of discourse analysis is "the compilation of all actual statements (spoken or written) in their historical dispersion and in their specific momentary value" (Foucault, 1970, p 155, author's translation). Discourse is "the always final and actually delimited body of precisely those linguistic sequences that have been formulated" (Foucault, 1970, p 156, author's translation). However, the discourse as this body of statements is not self-evident. It is the first task of the discourse analyst carefully to outline this body, in order to construct the *archive* as that which ultimately regulates what has been said and not been said in a given society. Naturally, it is impossible to decide in advance which discursive formation regulates the dispersion of particular statements. As a discourse analyst, it is necessary to travel the long and cautious road via the archive in order to approach the question of the shaping of specific discursive formations: "Only through a description of the archive of a discourse does it become possible to see the discursive formation as well as its *transformation*" (Ifversen, 1997, p 486). In Foucault's words: "One ought to read everything, study everything. In other words, one must have at one's disposal the general archive of a period at a given moment. And archaeology is, in a strict sense, the science of this archive" (Foucault, 1998a, p 263). Reading "everything" means a number of things to Foucault:

- First, it means that, since it is not possible to define the discursive formation beforehand, one cannot limit one's reading to a theme such as, for example, madness. Themes can relate to each other in unpredictable ways, which, moreover, can change over time and between spaces. We therefore have to follow the references of the statement and the references of the references in time and space in the broadest sense, until they appear to form a completed whole. There is no shortcut without consequences, as with the fate of the discourse commentator.
- Second, Foucault maintains that it does not suffice to read the canonical works pointed out by the history of ideas. It is crucial that the reading also includes the statements of the institutions, statements that demonstrate practice. Unravelling the history of madness includes readings of philosophical works as well as scientific dissertations and the statements, regulations and accounts of the institutions themselves.
- Third, and finally, we must be careful not to install a preconceived distinction between official and more private and individual sources, as if the private and personal sources exist outside the discourse.

For example...

In the studies by Foucault of the self-relation of the self, diaries and personal notes from Rome in the 1st and 2nd centuries play an important role in the analysis. Likewise, novels, paintings and personal documents appear as frequently used material. And, understandably, we cannot weigh up the types of statement against each other in advance, as if a text by Voltaire is of greater importance than documents written by an historically anonymous person, which, in turn, are more important than the diaries of a doctor, and so on.

Not until the archive has been established is it possible to inquire about the *discursive formations*. Not until the entire body of statements has been pieced together can we start to ask questions about the way one or more regularities appear in the irregular dispersion of statements, in other words, how the dispersion of statements over time seems to be regulated by different discursive formations. For Foucault it is about "seizing the statement in its momentary conciseness and total singularity, determining its exact boundaries, establishing the connections to other statements to which it can be linked, and showing which other categories of statements are thus excluded" (Foucault, 1970, p 156, author's translation). The fundamental question to the statements posed by discourse analysis in the attempt to create discursive formations is: 'Why did this and no other statement happen here?' (Foucault, 1970, p 156, author's translation). The aim is to detect the rules that govern the way different statements come into being in discursive formations. Rules in this context mean rules of acceptability, that is, rules about when a statement is accepted as a reasonable statement.

The formation of statements

Foucault distinguishes between four levels in a discursive formation, that is, four bodies of rules for the formation of statements (Foucault, 1986a, pp 21-71).

The formation of objects

The question here is why statements shape their objects the way they do.

- What is the regularity of the dispersed formation of objects by the statements?
- According to which rules are the objects created, ordered and classified?
- Which relations (for example, cause–effect relations) are established between the discursive objects?
- Which hierarchy of objects does the individual object form a part of?
- How are the objects specified and characterised?

These types of questions serve the purpose of isolating specific discursive formations and their rules for the formation of objects.

The formation of subjects

A discursive formation is a regulation of the dispersion of subject positions as they come into being in an individual statement. Here, the fundamental question is why the statements create subject positions the way they do. Discursive objects are always enunciated from a particular place – objects are always objects of a subject. Consequently, the question of subject positions is a question about the place from which the objects are enunciated.

- From which subject positions do the objects appear the way they do in the discourse?

This pertains to the rules of acceptability for the shaping of the spaces from which one can speak and observe in the discursive formation, but it also pertains to the existing rules for the acceptance of entering certain individuals into the spaces that are being created, and when this can happen. That is:

- Which qualities relate to subject positions?
- In which situation can the subject position be used as a platform for speaking and observing?
- What are the rules for observation and for the formation of statements when one assumes a specific position?

The formation of concepts

The enunciation of the subject positions and the discursive objects furthermore implies the connection to concepts. The questions are:

- Why does the statement actualise particular concepts and not others?
- How do concepts organise and connect statements?
- What are the rules for conceptualisation and how do specific discursive formations draw on concepts from other formations, including the rules of transcription, which seem to exist between different discursive formations?

The formation of strategies

A specific discursive formation is thus provisionally characterised by a particular creation of objects, subject positions and concepts. However, even in regard to the different levels of rules for the definition of formations, other objects could be enunciated, other subject positions could be established, other concepts could be actualised and linked together. Strategy is about rules of selection for the completion or actualisation of the rules of acceptability. Jan Ifversen attempts a formulation of these questions thus: "The potential possibilities of the discursive formation is narrowed down by virtue of 'strategic decisions'. In order to illustrate the appearance of a discursive formation, one needs to identify the limitations expressed by the strategic decision" (Ifversen, 1997, p 483). This question is by definition interdiscursive – it addresses how individual discursive formations always come into being in relation to other discursive formations.

This process involves a battle and competition, but also a mutual constitution between different discursive formations – a constellation that defines the conditions of the distribution of statements by the individual discursive formation. The inter-discursive relations need to be defined as they appear. They are defined through the individual discursive formations and their statements. Again, it is important to avoid any form of reductionism such as, for example, referring the inter-discursive competition to structures or conditions that do not appear explicitly in the competition, for example, economy, power, international regimes of production. The formulation of the rules of formation for strategies concerns the formulation of *the unity of the mutual exclusion of the discursive formations*. Foucault formulates it thus:

> One may describe between several discourses, relations of mutual delimitation, each giving the other distinctive marks of its singularity to be the differentiation of its domain of application. [...] This whole group of relations forms a principle of determination that permits or excludes, within a given discourse, a certain number of statements. These are conceptual systematizations, enunciative series, groups and organizations of objects that might have been possible (and of which nothing can justify the absence at the level of their own rules of formation), but which are excluded by a discursive constellation at a higher level and in a broader space. A discursive formation does not occupy therefore all the possible volume that is opened up to it right by the systems of formation of its object, its enunciations and its concepts; it is essentially incomplete, owing to the system of formation of its strategic choices. (Foucault, 1986a, p 67)

Conclusion

Accordingly, the regulating difference in the analytical strategy of the knowledge archaeology is regularity/dispersion of statements. The archaeological eye divides the world into dispersed statements and the regularity of the dispersion. In fact, that is all there is. The remaining concepts serve the sole purpose of defining when a statement can be regarded as a statement and when regularity can be regarded as regular. Discursive formations are analysed as regularities of dispersion of statements in which statements are seen as events possessing certain functions of existence, which produce objects, subjects, conceptual networks and strategies.

Genealogy

Genealogical analysis cannot be separated from archaeological analysis. The relation between archaeology and genealogy is frequently portrayed, in Foucault, as two periods in his writings in which the genealogical breakthrough is summoned with the article 'Nietzsche – genealogy and history' (Foucault, 1991). However, before this publication Foucault had already used the term 'genealogy', at times together with the word 'archaeology'. Moreover, the majority of the questions addressed in the Neitzsche article had already been discussed before in *The archaeology of knowledge* (Foucault, 1986a), in the chapter 'Discourse and discontinuity', and in different introductory problem formulations in his historical works. In this section, I will construe the genealogical analytical strategy as the historical dimension of the knowledge archaeology. Consequently it is impossible, in my understanding, to conduct a knowledge-archaeological analysis without combining it with a genealogical analysis. In my exposition, the following is chosen as my starting point.

Framework for genealogical analysis

Whereas the framework for the eye of knowledge archaeology is the difference regularity/dispersion of statements, the framework for the eye of genealogy is the difference continuity/discontinuity.

The designation of genealogy as a particular historical analytical strategy was initially developed by Friedrich Nietzsche, primarily in his dissertation *On the genealogy of morality* (Nietzsche, 1998). In this text, Nietzsche explains how he began by looking into the origins of good and evil but how he gradually realised that this way of asking was tremendously problematic because of the question's implied supposition about an original essential moral that would appear increasingly clear as one approached its source on tracing it back through history.

Nietzsche redefines his question and thus ascribes to it the characteristics of genealogy. He asks:"Under what conditions did man invent those value judgements good and evil? *And what value do they themselves have?*" (Nietzsche, 1998, pp 2-3). The genealogy of morals subsequently revolves around "the conditions and circumstances out of which [these values] have grown, under which they have developed and shifted" (p 5). The aim becomes to question the value of values in all facets. The genealogy of morals is also therefore a *critique of morality*.

The genealogical analytical strategy is defined in opposition to traditional historiography. In the genealogical analytical strategy, Foucault assumes Nietzsche's critique of history in which Nietzsche distinguishes between three methods of historiography.

The monumental method

This historiography cultivates the connections and continuity of greatness of all times. Monumental history harmonises heterogeneity, generalises and, conclusively, analogises. It is all but critical: it deceives and seduces through analogies and leads to rashness (Nietzsche, 1988). National history is a classic example of this. Other, more current, examples could be various histories about our path toward globalisation, or books about the formation of the idea of Europe, which is now unfolding through the European Union. But it might also be books about the historical progress of medical science or the dissemination of modern humanism and its repression of the barbaric means of punishment of earlier times.

The antiquarian method

Antiquarian historiography cultivates the past for the sake of the past. It becomes a blinded collection mania and a restless amassing of things of the past. Such a historiography mummifies life; it is incapable of breeding life and always underestimates the future (Nietzsche, 1988).

The critical method

This historiography stands in the service of life. Critical historiography has, as its starting point, the notion that the past must be broken up and annulled in order to allow the living to exist. The past must be held accountable, submitted to awkward interrogations and convicted – not in order to achieve justice or mercy, but in order to allow for the emergence of life and force (Nietzsche, 1988).

The fundamental distinction in Nietzsche's critique of history is whether the historiography stands in the service of life or death. The antiquarian operates in the service of death, exclusively through his mummified historiography. Monumental historiography is more ambiguous: it provides people with a future prospect that enables them to act and perform, but it leads to rashness because it presents the future in the singular, as necessary and inevitable. Critical historiography alone is in the service of life, by providing an opening in which the past locks us up in presuppositions and morals. Knowledge about the past is not in itself beneficial; on the contrary, says Nietzsche, we need to forget in order to live. Robert Scharff sums it up thus:

> What Nietzsche's first generation opponent of history chooses to do is reject the conception of past, future, and present that inform historical science: at some decisive point, he must forget rather than remember more and more of the past. He must turn away from rather than survey the whole process, so that the future looks open instead of finished in anticipation. And the less he presently knows of the whole, the younger he feels. (Scharff, 1974, p 74)

Regularity and discontinuity

According to Allan Megill, Foucault maintains this distinction between the historiography of life and death. Megill refers to the tension between Apollo (the god of knowledge, the arts, order and civilisation) and Dionysus (the god of wine, mysteries, darkness and death) as a fundamental tension in Foucault's analytical-strategic development (Megill, 1979, p 459). In Foucault's work, this tension appears as the tension between archaeology as the systematic analytical strategy (Apollonian) concerned with the regularity of the irregular, and genealogy as an analytical strategy, concerned with discontinuity, which brings on life and undermines presuppositions (Dionysian). Foucault hence tries to extend the Dionysian thinking in his genealogies. According to Foucault, genealogy comprises three critical forms of application that serve life:

1. *Reality-destructive use*, which opposes the historical motif recollection-recognition. Foucault's historiography is reality-destructive when, as in *Madness and civilization*, it challenges the way the present recognises itself in its historical texts.
2. *Identity-destructive use*, which opposes the historical motif continuity-tradition. Foucault's historiography is identity-destructive, when, as in *Discipline and punish*, it denounces the humanist identity by showing that the history of punishment does not consist in one unbroken movement towards a humanisation of the penalty system since the Middle Ages, but, conversely, that modern means of punishment indicate an intensification of punishment because the aim is no longer simply to torment the body but also to control the psyche. Foucault thus employs history in order to undermine the humanist complacency of the present. He wants the professional practitioners of humanism in the institutions to feel uncomfortable. Foucault says of the identity-destructive application of genealogy: "The purpose of history, guided by genealogy, is not to discover the roots of our identity, but to commit itself to its dissipation" (Foucault, 1991, p 95).
3. *Truth-destructive use*, which opposes the historical motif of knowledge. This applies to Foucault's critique of psychology and psychoanalysis when he demonstrates, for example, how the truth about insanity can never be found in psychology, for the simple reason that the truth about insanity is located in the very society that is responsible for creating the conditions of the origin of insanity and madness. Foucault says, in regard to the truth-destructive use of genealogy, "all knowledge rests upon injustice" (Foucault, 1991). He concludes that the goal is to create in history a counter-memory (Foucault, 1991, p 93).

The purpose of genealogy, for Foucault, is not therefore a description of actual events. Genealogy is a history of the present designed to outline the historical conflicts and strategies of control by which knowledge and discourses are constituted and operate, and to use these descriptions as a counter-memory.

Foucault is concerned with the redescription of "not the anticipatory power of meaning, but the hazardous play of dominations" (Foucault, 1991, p 83).

> Genealogy does not pretend to go back in time to restore an unbroken continuity that operates beyond the dispersion of broken things; its duty is not to demonstrate that the past actively exists in the present, that it continues secretly to animate the present, having imposed a predetermined form on all its vicissitudes. (Foucault, 1991, p 81)

Rather, the aim is to query the discourses and practices of the present by referring them back to the hegemonic conditions under which they have been established, which also includes pointing out ruptures in the grounds on which strategies, institutions and practices are shaped. The presuppositions of the present are to be dissolved by means of history[2]. Mats Beronius sums up the main task of genealogy:

> Instead of analysing an event, a phenomenon, or the history of an idea by looking for the governing idea and leitmotif which should link together the source and result of history, the analyst should attempt to draw the different and multifaceted branches of a genealogical tree. [...] To trace the origin of a social phenomenon (an institution, a practice, an idea etc) does not imply the establishing of the birth of the phenomenon, but rather the tracing of its line of descent. (Beronius, 1991, pp 50-2, author's translation)

Foucault himself formulates it thus:

> The isolation of different points of emergence does not conform to the successive configurations of an identical meaning; rather, they result from substitutions, displacements, disguised conquests, and systematic reversals. If interpretation were the slow exposure of the meaning hidden in an origin, then only metaphysics could interpret the development of humanity. But if interpretation is the violent or surreptitious appropriation of a system of rules, which in itself has no essential meaning, in order to impose a direction, to bend it to a new will, to force its participation in a different game, and to subject it to secondary rules, then the development of humanity is a series of interpretations. The role of genealogy is to record its history: the history of morals, ideals, and metaphysical concepts, the history of the concept of liberty or of the ascetic life; as they stand for the emergence of different interpretations, they must be made to appear as events on the stage of historical process. (Foucault, 1991, p 86)

Here, the continuity and discontinuity of difference is a tool for observation, employed in order to distinguish discontinuity in that which presents itself as continuity and to examine possible continuities in that which presents itself as new, different or unique. The genealogical method is concerned with the continued openness of the object. Instead of a preliminary definition of the object of our examination, we need to investigate *how* our object has been construed historically in different ways and in different settings. We are not only to look for those events that stand out clearly as seen from the present, but also for those constructions, strategies and practices that, for some reason, never distinguished themselves, disintegrated or changed into something else. Hence, we should not just trace that which became history, but also very much that which has been defined as mistakes, antiquated, unrealistic and so on. In this respect, the approach needs to be wide rather than deep. The way of seeing that the difference continuity/discontinuity constitutes is a *glance of dissociation,*

> a glance that distinguishes, separates, and disperses; that is capable of liberating divergence and marginal elements – the kind of dissociating view that is capable of decomposing itself, capable of shattering the unity of man's being through which it was thought that he could extend his sovereignty to the events of his past. (Foucault, 1991, p 87)

Figure 1.1 attempts to illustrate the genealogical analytical strategy.

Here, the objective is to trace the lines of descent of psychoanalysis. Each circle expresses a discursive strategy or an institutional practice. Each letter expresses discursive or institutional elements, which are part of a strategic or institutional order. The lines illustrate the relationships between discursive formations and practices. A relationship requires at least one element to be carried on in a subsequent formation or practice. As discursive formation and practice, psychoanalysis has thus come into being through a transformation of elements from a multitude of formations and practices, including the Catholic practice of confession, the hospital and the internment institution. Genealogy can be used to illustrate, for one thing, how psychoanalysis both repeats and

Figure 1.1: The genealogy of psychoanalysis

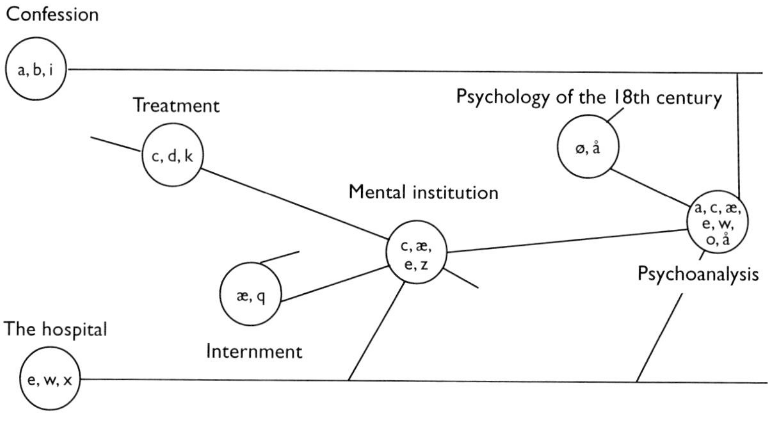

Source: This figure is a slightly altered version of a figure from Noujain, 1987.

renews a control issue pertaining to the handling of deviants, but which has obtained a specific definition and elaboration within the individual formations and practices.

For example...

One example of these specific definitions and elaborations of the control issue is the Poor Law internment institution, in which poor people, criminals and people with mental illness were locked up together and excluded from ordinary life and from the rest of society, to hide these examples of unwanted, non-industrious laziness. Later examples are the mental institutions, in which mad people were distinguished as a particular group and notions of societal dependency were impressed on them in their treatment, as discussed above. Finally, there is psychoanalysis, which introduces the distinction between the body and the consciousness of the 'madman' and aims to restore his communication with the outside world (Foucault, 1971).

Genealogy provides no explanations of causality. The lines of descent are not causal, for example 'at first, there were hospitals, which were further developed in the mental institution, which led to the development of psychoanalysis'. The lines of descent simply imply an *originating affiliation*, that is, that psychoanalysis ties together and transforms elements from previous discursive strategies and practices in its own process of construction. Moreover, there is no simple seriality in which discursive strategies successively supersede each other. Conversely, a new strategy can easily emanate through the transformation of elements from a specific discursive formation while this strategy is sustained. It is even probable that the 'first' discursive strategy survives the 'offspring'.

The endpoint of genealogy determines which discourses and discursive kinships one discovers. A minor displacement of the endpoint is therefore able to alter history quite significantly. The focus could, for example, be on hospitals rather than psychoanalysis and this could identify new and central moments that might also involve significant relationships to psychoanalysis, which would otherwise have been overlooked, for example the medical way of seeing.

This does not mean, however, that discursive histories are fictional in the sense that it is entirely open which stories can be told. Rather, it means that no history can be described without being rooted in problem and perspective. History is a constructed reality of a perspective and is real and observable as such. This question is unfolded frequently in Foucault's work, for example in relation to periodisation:

Every periodization carves out in history a certain level of events, and, conversely, each layer of events calls for its own periodization. This is a set of delicate problems, since, depending on the level that one selects, one will have to delimit different periodizations, and depending on the periodization one provides, one will reach different levels. In this way one arrives at the complex methodology of discontinuity. (Foucault, 1998a, p 284)

This, of course, has implications for the reading and analysis of the different monuments of history, such as texts, images, legal reports and so on. The displacement of one's perspective and problem changes not only what one sees, but also the way of seeing employed when reading and analysing. It changes the statements to which one's attention is drawn as well as the connections one sees between statements:

> The texts that I spoke of could easily be taken up again, along with the very material that I treated, in a description that would have a different periodization and would be situated at a different level. For example, when the archaeology of historical knowledge is done, obviously it will be necessary to again use the texts on language, and it will be necessary to relate them to the techniques of exegesis, of the criticism of sources, and to all the knowledge concerning sacred scripture and the historical tradition. Their description will be different then. But if they are exact, these descriptions should be such that one can define the transformations that make it possible to go from one to the other. (Foucault, 1998a, p 284)

Again, as Foucault points out, this does not lead to relativism but rather perspectivism. Given a specific perspective and problem, genealogy becomes sensitive to its material in a specific way. However, genealogical descriptions can be criticised for their perspective. Naturally, it is always possible to take a step back and investigate the relevance and probability of a particular perspective and problem, thus questioning all criteria of selection and the validity of the examination.

In the same way that archaeology is concerned with statements as they appear, avoiding any form of discourse commentary, a similar phenomenological antireductionism is stressed in genealogy. Foucault maintains that genealogy must be unobtrusive and:

> record the singularity of events outside of any monotonous finality; it must seek them in the most unpromising places, in what we tend to feel is without history – in sentiments, love, conscience, instincts; it must be sensitive to their recurrence, not in order to trace the gradual curve of their evolution, but to isolate the different scenes where they engaged in different roles. Finally, genealogy must define even those instances when they are absent, the moment when they remained unrealised (Plato, at Syracuse, did not become Mohammed). (Foucault, 1991, p 76)

He emphasises that genealogy is "gray, meticulous, and patiently documentary. It operates on a field of entangled and confused parchments, on documents that have been scratched over and recopied many times" (Foucault, 1991, p 76).

Self-technology analysis

Knowledge archaeology and genealogy are among the most clearly described analytical strategies in the writings of Foucault, but there are a number of others. Self-technology analysis concerns the analysis of the technologies available to an individual's manifestation of itself as subject. Whereas knowledge-archaeological discourse analysis allows for studies of the way in which subject positions are created, the analysis of self-technologies permits studies of the practical staging of the relationship between individual and subject position.

At an early stage in his writings, Foucault spoke of practice as something that does not unambiguously coincide with discourse. His understandings of practice, however, remain unclear, although he seems to border on directions for practice. In relation to the history of sexuality, the concept of practice appears to be replaced by the concept of technology, although this replacement is not unambiguous. What *is* unambiguous, in turn, is the question posed by means of the concept of technology – it pertains to the self-relation of the subject to its self-care.

In his sociology, Simmel defines a distinction between position and vocation as two different ways in which a person can become an individual. Similarly, Foucault distinguishes between subjection and subjectivation (for example, Foucault, 1997, 1998b; and Balibar, 1994). To Foucault, *subjection* means that an individual or collective is proclaimed subject within a specific discourse. The individual or collective is offered a specific position in the discourse from which one can speak and act meaningfully in a specific way. Foucault speaks of *subjectivation* when the individual or collective has not only been made the subject but also *wishes* to be so. Subjection, thus, signifies the space where one *receives oneself*, whereas subjectivation signifies the space where one *gives oneself to oneself* (Schmidt, 1990).

This distinction is not merely theoretical. It is also a distinction between two forms of discursive demands on the person who is to become the subject: a distinction between two modes of subjection. The appropriation by the individual of a subject position is not observable in terms of discourse analysis. It is, however, observable whether and how the discourse demands active self-appropriation of a subject position. This is exactly what Foucault discovered in the history of sexuality – the fact that the individual is not only required to fill out a particular subject position but also to care for her/himself independently. The interesting point is that the discourse itself, through the subjecting of the individual, makes a distinction between subjecting and subjectivation in which the former forms a counter-concept in relation to the latter. As it is, demands are made on the individual not to simply receive oneself passively but actively to give oneself to oneself. In that sense, the aforementioned mode of subjecting is a *mode of transformation* – it invokes the passively receiving and subjected so that s/he may cross the line from subjection to subjectivation, thereby making her/himself actively sovereign in her/his own self-creation. It is an invocation to the individual to invoke her/himself.

The question is then how this self-transformation comes about. Foucault opens up the question in his study of self-care by introducing technology as mediation. Foucault distinguishes between four types of technology: production technologies, sign technologies, power technologies and self-technologies. He sees the latter as technologies that allow for individuals to influence operations that concern their own body, soul, thoughts, control and mode of existence, so that they are able to transform themselves and achieve a specific state of happiness, purity, wisdom, perfection or immortality (Foucault, 1997). In other words, self-technologies are procedures that prescribe how the individual is to define, maintain and develop her/his identity with a view to self-control and self-awareness (Foucault, 1997). The purpose of these technologies is for the self to address itself.

Foucault gracefully skips over how to perceive of technology generally. He defines four criteria in relation to self-technology:

1. The transformational mode of subjecting.
2. The objectification of the self.
3. Self-activating activity.
4. Telos.

These criteria also define the basic question through which we will examine the technologies (see also, Davidson, 1986; Hacking, 1986).

Figure 1.2: The elements of self-technology

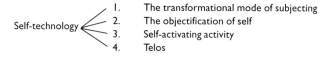

Self-technology	1.	The transformational mode of subjecting
	2.	The objectification of self
	3.	Self-activating activity
	4.	Telos

1. The transformational mode of subjecting

The first criterion of technology is the fact that it is a transformational mode of subjecting, that is, that the individual is called on to give itself to itself. The question is:

• How is the individual subjected with a view to crossing the boundary between subjecting/subjectivation?

2. The objectification of the self

The second criterion is the objectification of the self, which concerns the form of knowledge that the individual can establish about itself as self. The question is:

- As *what* is the self to master itself? Is the self to master itself as feeling, as desire, as will, or as culture?

3. Self-activating activity

The third criterion is the stipulations for self-activating activities, for example, the diary as self-activity that emerged in the 2nd century in the Roman Empire (Foucault, 1997), or the confessional practice of the Catholic Church. Examples of modern technologies could be the 'time manager' of the 1980s or competence interviews in the workplace.

4. Telos

Finally, the fourth criterion is the fact that the self-activity needs to have a direction or an aim that extends beyond the mere activity. The question is:

- In what way does the self-technology provide the individual with a particular telos for life?

Conclusion

Self-technology can therefore be understood as prescriptions for operations through which the individual, having received itself through subjecting, is able to reach a point of transformation so that it can give itself to itself in order to obtain a particular personal goal or condition. In that way, self-technologies are defined as technologies through which the individual can transform itself from a state of having responsibilities into taking on responsibilities, which means that the individual puts her/his own development on the agenda and accepts responsibility for it.

This understanding of self-technology analysis thus divides the world into subjecting and subjectivation, and constructs a sensitivity to the practices through which the self can summon itself and activate itself in order to master its own creation. The concept of 'subjecting', which was a subconcept in archaeological discourse analysis, increases in importance and becomes one aspect of the fundamental analytical way of seeing.

Dispositive analysis

The final analytical strategy of Foucault, which I will briefly discuss, is dispositive analysis. Dispositive analysis is quite difficult to describe and Foucault's systematic descriptions of the analysis are very limited. Nevertheless, it is a central analytical strategy, particularly in *Discipline and punish* (1977) and *History of sexuality* (1978). Most works on Foucault have disregarded dispositive analysis and have focused on archaeology and genealogy; those who have addressed dispositive analysis have described it very differently. Gilles Deleuze describes dispositive as a structuring of light composed by lines of different nature (Deleuze, 1992), Neil Brenner as a functional imperative (Brenner, 1994), and Mitchell Dean as a regime of practices (Dean, 1999, p 21).

What makes dispositive analysis difficult to grasp is the fact that it can only be perceived as a complementary analytical strategy, which succeeds the archaeology, genealogy and self-technology analyses. These analytical strategies are preconditions of dispositive analysis because the focus of dispositive analysis is precisely the interconnections between different discourses, institutions, practices, self-technologies, tactics and so on, within a particular period. Foucault defines dispositive as:

1. "a thoroughly heterogeneous ensemble consisting of discourses, institutions, architectural forms, regulatory decisions, laws, administrative measures, scientific statements, philosophical, moral and philanthropic propositions";
2. "the nature of connections that can exist between these heterogeneous elements'";
3. "a strategic imperative" (Foucault, 1980, pp 194-5).

Whereas archaeology divides the world into the regulation and dispersion of statements, geneaology into continuity and discontinuity, and self-technology analysis into subjection and subjectivation, dispositive analysis divides the world into *apparatus* on one hand and *strategic logic* on the other hand. The distinction between apparatus and strategic logic is the 'eye' of dispositive analysis.

The apparatus is the 'heterogeneous ensemble'; it is a system of elements between which there exists a functional connection. The strategic imperative or logic is a generalised schematic that brings about a particular logic. These are always relative in relation to one another. There is no apparatus without the apparatus acting as an apparatisation and, thus, a function of a strategic logic. In turn, there is no strategic logic except through the effects it defines through an apparatus. I have attempted to outline dispositive analysis in Figure 1.3.

Generalisation

This analysis is in fact a 'two-in-one' analytical strategy, since Foucault oscillates between viewing the problem from the side of the apparatus and the side of the strategy respectively of the guiding distinction. When indicating the side

Figure 1.3: Dispositive analysis

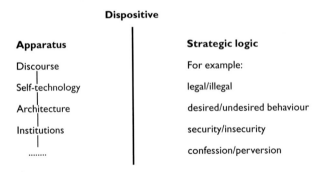

'strategy' of the distinction, Foucault examines the way in which a discursive element is taken out of the specific context in which it was created, and is then generalised and given schematic qualities so that it is made available as logic to a multiplicity of discourses, self-technologies, institutions and so on. For example, Foucault examines how specific laws are generalised within the schematic of legal/illegal, which deals with its surrounding environment according to very specific procedures. Or the way discipline is generalised within the schematic of desired/undesired with a functionality that concerns the prevention of the undesired before it occurs, subjecting its environment to a particular disciplining. Or how specific actions in the army are generalised within the schematic of security/insecurity with a functionality about being prepared for the unexpected, and preventing negative effects and maybe even turning them to an advantage (Raffnsøe, 2000, p 58).

These generalisations always mean that the specific technology or discursive element is taken out of its specific context and becomes a strategic logic that can be installed into many more contexts than just the one that produced it.

For example...

Foucault speaks of the 'prisonisation' of society, thus pointing to how the logic of discipline, which is born out of a context of surveillance and punishment, is generalised so that it can subsequently obtain meaning in educational systems, workplaces, and so on.

Apparatisation

On the other hand, when indicating the side of the apparatus in the guiding distinction, the question is how a particular strategic logic is brought about through apparatisation, in which forms, such as discourses, technologies and architectures, are linked as functional elements in a system.

For example...

One possible question is:

- How are elements linked together to form an educational system in a particular way when the logic of discipline is formed?

We have schools that divide students according to age, divide space into classrooms and divide time into lessons. We have architectural forms that construct classrooms with peepholes so that the class does not know if or when it is being observed by the principal.

The two analytical movements are illustrated in Figure 1.4.

The study of generalisation is therefore about becoming aware of the strategic logics brought about by technologies, discourses, self-technologies, rites, decisions, practical arrangements and so on. It is important not to perceive the strategic logics teleologically: they serve no purpose that extends beyond themselves. They establish a kind of intention and direction without concrete content and programme, and without a particular will or subjectivity. The logic is an abstract intentionality, defined solely by a schematic (for example, desired+/undesired–), with a basic motivation and strategy without subject and content. What is lacking in the strategic logics, with respect to content, will and programme, must be provided by the apparatus.

By contrast, the study of the apparatisation of the logic concerns the way in which these logics are brought about through linking elements in an apparatus, and how the actual creation of the apparatus specifies and programmes the unfolding of the logics. In the study of the apparatisation, it is important to be aware of at least four conditions:

Figure 1.4: The double movement of dispositive analysis

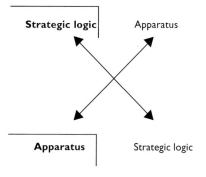

| Strategic logic | Apparatus | How are discursive or technological elements generalised into a schematic, which forms a specific strategic logic? |

| Apparatus | Strategic logic | How are forms linked as functional elements in an apparatus that brings about a specific strategic logic? |

- First, the elements of discourse and self-technology must have been constructed as objects in preceding archaeological discourse analysis and self-technology analysis before they can be studied as 'functional elements-in-an-apparatus'. Thus, it is the discourse analysis and not the dispositive analysis that constructs the individual discourse through its awareness of the regularity in the dispersion of statements. Because of this, I find it difficult to perceive of dispositive analysis as more than an extension of a number of logically preceding analyses.
- Second, an apparatisation of a particular strategic logic is not constructed 'from scratch'. Self-technologies, knowledge, institutions and so on will often have previously formed part of other apparatuses. Apparatisation, thus, is often about the way elements are *re*installed with new relational functions in the bringing about of other logics.
- Third, it is possible for several logics to be involved in the creation of an apparatus. It is an element of the analysis of an apparatisation to examine both how the logic is deflected by the functional elements that are linked together in a specific apparatus and also how different logics deflect each other within the same apparatus. If we again take the school as an example, it does not only become an apparatisation of the logic of discipline; the logic of law is also imprinted in the school and deflects the logic of discipline by permitting and prohibiting certain disciplining technologies.
- Fourth, Foucault is highly aware of the fact that no apparatisation takes place without counter-power also moving into the apparatuses in the shape of forms and elements that cannot be absorbed by strategic logics. Neil Brenner even suggests an understanding of the question of counter-power as a Foucauldian version of dysfunctionality (Brenner, 1994).

Conclusion

In conclusion, we see in Foucault at least four different analytical strategies, each constituted on their guiding distinction. Genealogical analysis seeks, by a gaze of disruption, to open up the discursive field through tracing practices, discourses and institutional lines of descent, including the lines of connection to different historical conflicts and strategies of control. Archaeological analytical strategy, in turn, seeks to describe discourses as regularities in the dispersion of statements, including the displacement over time of these regularities. Together they form an analytical strategy that is designed to evoke formation and transformation. Self-technology analysis attempts to capture the ways in which an individual can give itself to itself. Finally, there is dispositive analysis, which inquires, as a layer on top of the other analytical strategies, about how discursive and extra-discursive elements are linked together in an apparatus in the bringing about of a particular strategic logic.

I have attempted to encapsulate these analytical strategies in Table 1.1. The left-hand column indicates the analytical strategies; the centre column tries to capture the particular way of inquiring of each strategy; the right-hand column provides a concrete example of how a specific social issue can be discussed, based on Foucault, and what the differences are depending on which of Foucault's analytical strategies is employed.

The example used here pertains to the development of the relationship between employee and organisation. Over the past 20 years, the construction and definition of the employee has been put on the agenda. The relationships between individual and role has been addressed. Employees' personal lives have been integrated into the workplace. Staff policies have become life policies with management speak including terms such as 'lifelong learning', 'flexibility', 'personal competencies', the 'complete human being'. New practices, such as performance and competence reviews, have come to prevail.

Table 1.1: Foucault's analytical strategies

Analytical strategy	General question	Example
Archaeological discourse analysis	Why did this and not another statement occur in this place?	In what way has a new discourse been established that articulates the employee as a complete and responsible human being with responsibility for his or her own development?
Genealogy	How are different discursive formations and discursive strategies shaped and transformed?	In what way does the new discourse about the complete employee not simply express a humanisation of the workplace, but also an internationalization of previous forms of discipline
Self-technology analysis	How have self-technologies been created and how do they prescribe the way an individual can give itself to itself?	How are performance and competence reviews developed and carried out as self-technologies, through which the employee can learn to master himself as strategic resource in the workplace?
Dispositive analysis	How are forms linked together as functional elements of an apparatus? How are discursive or technological elements generalised in a schematic that develops a strategic logic?	In what way does the educational way of seeing become a general schematic and strategy for organising, and how is the educational scheme propagated and apparatised in employee discourses, self-technologies, office architecture, and so on?

As it is hopefully clear from Table 1.1, the choice of analytical strategy makes an important difference to one's empirical and problem-related sensitivity:

- Archaeology illuminates the emergence and regimental character of the discourse.
- Genealogy gives insight into the displacement of disciplinary forms.
- Self-technology analysis highlights the ways of ordering of the new practices.
- Dispositive analysis makes one aware of the logics that unfold through the new technologies, practices and institutions, and how these are linked together in an apparatus.

Notes

[1] My exposition of *The order of things* draws on Raffnsøe, 1999.

[2] For a further discussion of Foucault's genealogy, see for example, Megill, 1979; Roth, 1981; Shiner, 1982; Kent, 1986; Mahon, 1992.

Reinhart Koselleck's history of concepts

R einhart Koselleck's history of concepts probably represents the clearest breakthrough of the linguistic turn within historical science. Koselleck's history of concepts was developed at end of the 1950s and, since then, has become an extensive programme for the study of the rise of modernity. The programme studies the origins of a great number of concepts, particularly political and administrative ones, in connection with the effects of their social history. This has resulted in a comprehensive encyclopaedia in eight volumes of the history of concepts entitled *Geschichtliche Grundbegriffe, Historisches Lexikon zur politisch-sozialen Sprache in Deutschland* (Brunner et al, 1972). The encyclopaedia includes concepts such as 'politics', 'citizen', 'public', 'nature', 'interest', 'representation', 'administration' and 'tyranny'.

Jan Ifversen (1997) characterises the history of concepts as a linguistic turn *within* the discipline of social history. Although the history of concepts has developed as an indication of limitations and problems in traditional social history, it has never proclaimed itself to be a new, radical, historical science in opposition to all traditional historiography. The history of concepts has therefore been able to develop without a destructive conflict with the less theoretical historical sciences. On the contrary, the history of concepts has commanded respect from traditional historians, while Foucault's discourse-analytical historiography has never obtained recognition within traditional historical disciplines. The history of concepts has been seen and has seen itself as a niche within historical science, but not until recently has conceptual historical thinking extended beyond the encyclopaedia to which it is rooted. This shift is particularly visible in Scandinavia in the work of historians such as Bo Stråht, Henrik Sidenius and Kari Palonnen (see for example, Stråht, 1990).

This chapter focuses only on Koselleck's history of concepts. There have been other attempts at writing the history of concepts, but from the discourse-analysis perspective, Koselleck's contribution is of the greatest interest (see for example, Pocock, 1987; Tully, 1988; Richter, 1990, 1995). As Ifversen points out (1997), the other efforts often do not reach beyond assumptions in respect of conceptual history. For example, Quentin Skinner (1984), despite an intention to do the opposite, remains located in the history of ideas, focusing on canonical works without regard for more anonymous texts (such as administrative texts) and without regard for those semantic or discursive fields of which the canonical works form a part (Ifversen and Østergård, 1996, p 25).

The relevance of the history of concepts can be summed up in three characteristics:

1. It presents a serious, anti–essentialist and constructivist challenge to traditional historiography.
2. It is founded on a reasonably simple theoretical apparatus that has not yet been unfolded, but which, in turn, has proved to be extremely sensitive to the empirical, exceedingly operational and analytically powerful.
3. It has succeeded in functioning on two different levels at once by writing the history of individual concepts, their origins, transformation and effects on social and political practices, as well as combining these individual histories in a joined description of the transformation of political semantics in the notion of *neuzeit* (neuzeit is the designation by historians of concepts of the transition from premodernity to modernity).

Origins of the history of concepts

The fundamental premise for the history of concepts is the idea that concepts are central to the constitution of society, including the constitution of action as well as agents of action. The shaping of concepts is hence not a simple surface phenomenon. If historical science is indeed seeking to raise critical constitutional questions, it must do so by defining the shaping of concepts as the central issue. Without concepts, notes Koselleck, there is no society and no political fields of action (Koselleck, 1982, p 410). This does not imply that everything can be reduced to concepts. According to Koselleck, the history of concepts must include linguistic as well as sociohistorical data – any semantics entail non-linguistic content (Koselleck, 1982, p 414). (We will return to this point in connection with the notion of concept later in this chapter.)

The constitution of society can therefore be examined as a semantic battle about the political and social; a battle about the definition, defence and occupation of conceptually composed positions. Concepts must be perceived of as reaching into the future: "Concepts no longer merely serve to define given states of affairs, they reach into the future. Increasingly concepts of the future were created, positions that were to be won had to be first linguistically formulated before it was possible to even enter or permanently occupy them" (Koselleck, 1982, pp 413-14).

Included in this proposition is the notion that semantics change at a slower pace than the events themselves. There are several factors related to this point:

- First, the fact that semantics, as a repository of articulated experience, contains the conditions of *possible* events. Semantics anticipate possible events but not their necessity.

- Second, the fact that the possible ways of semantic expression are limited gives it a more enduring stability. The semantic units (concepts) outlive the occasions comprised by the history of events:

    When new experience becomes, as it were, a part of language's inventory, as in the case of the centuries-old but ever more nuanced debate about the constitutions, or in the perennially recurring conflict between different notions of might and right, then the semantics has a slower rate of change than the events themselves. (Koselleck, 1989, p 657)

- Third, precisely because the concepts possess a different inner time structure than the events they participate in inciting or conceiving of, they are marked by perseverance in respect to their epoch, which turns semantics into an obvious historical object.

Knowledge interests

The purpose of the history of concepts is not merely to add yet another object to the historical sciences. The purpose is to examine the way in which the shaping of concepts and the transformation of the semantic fields move history and reach into *our* future. Koselleck criticises the kind of historical science that devotes itself exclusively to the study of individual incidents on the assumption that detailed studies of incidents are less problematic than studies of the structural history of longitudinal lines. Koselleck demonstrates how the narrative content of structures and events is fundamentally the same. Incidents are always construed narratively as events and, moreover, any event-oriented historical science is too meagre and is unable to contribute to a historical diagnosis of potential futures (Koselleck, 1985, pp 105-15).

The history of concepts also distinguishes between diachronic and synchronous analysis. Diachronic analysis consists of an analysis of the historical origins and transformation of individual concepts, and thus suggests a notion of concept. Synchronous analysis consists of an analysis of the semantic field in which concepts appear and connect with other concepts. Synchronous analysis frequently refers to concepts such as the 'semantic field', 'semantic structure' and 'counter-concepts'. I will further address these two conceptual sets below; however, initially I wish to stress that, to Koselleck, there can be no qualified history of concepts without both of them. The concept-historical analysis must continually move back and forth between the diachronic and the synchronous in order neither to fall back on a barren history of words nor forwards onto the pitiless social history of concepts.

The notion of concept

What is, then, Koselleck's notion of concept? First, it must be emphasised that, to Koselleck, concepts hold the very key to the unfolding of the *space of signification* of which experience and expectations form a part (Ifversen, 1997, p 448). The central concept is not discourse, statement or sentence, but concept alone, and this indicates one of the main differences between the notion of concept and many other discursive traditions such as those of Foucault and Laclau, for example.

Accordingly, concepts provide the portal to studies of the historical space of signification. But,

- What, then, is a concept?

Koselleck highlights the importance of distinguishing between word and concept in order not to depart into a history of mere words. Subsequently, he unfolds his notion of concept in a triad composed by word (that is, designation), meaning (that is, concept) and object (that is, fact) (Koselleck, 1972):

> Each concept is associated with a word, but not every word is a social and political concept. Social and political concepts possess a substantial claim of generality and always have many meanings. (Koselleck, 1982, p 418)

The distinctions between words, concepts and facts serve to define an autonomous space for the concept. Concepts are tied to words, but they are not one with the words; concepts refer to facts, but they are not identical to the facts, because the concepts provide the surroundings with meaning – not the reverse.

The difference between words and concepts revolves around the ability of words to work *unambiguously* in practical usage.

For example...

There are several meanings to the word 'tramp', but when used it is unambiguous. If someone gives advice to a potential boyfriend – "Stay clear of Sheila. She is a tramp" – the meaning is clear.

Conversely, a concept has to remain ambiguous, even when applied, in order to continue to be a concept – concepts are always fundamentally *ambiguous*.

For example...

One example is the concept of 'equality', which is never completely defined and can signify many things, from equal pay, minority issues and ethnic equality, to the struggle against the patriarch or the concept of 'the state' (which involves a range of elements such as territory, power, tax collection, jurisdiction). Or it may signify the concept of 'ecological sustainability' (which may include eco-balance or the relationship between economic growth and the environment). This concept functions as a point of reference to environmental bureaucrats as well as a utopia to dedicated environmentalists; it signifies both the good life and a pragmatic balancing of ecology and economy.

Koselleck specifies the construction in this way: "The meaning of a word can be determined exactly through definition, concepts can only be interpreted" (Koselleck, 1972, p XXIII, author's translation).

According to Koselleck, words become concepts through the condensation of a wide range of social and political meanings. Thus, concepts comprise an undecided abundance of meaning, a concentration of meaning, which makes them ambiguous. Without this ambiguity, concepts would not be capable of reaching into the future but, precisely because of its ambiguity, the concept reveals a space of signification that is open to interpretation and can become a semantic battlefield. Precisely through its ambiguity, the concept can create positions for later occupation and conquest, create time and space and so on. Without the ambiguity of concepts, there are simply no conditions of conceptual disagreement. If we were able to define 'equality', 'ecological sustainability', 'freedom', 'responsibility', 'representation', there would be no politics, no semantic battle and, consequently, no history. It is the concept of equality that organises the fight for equality as a struggle about reducing ambiguity and establishing positions from which equality can be represented. Historically, we can observe how various meanings have been condensed into the concept of equality and, thus, have organised the struggle for equality. Equality initially was taken to mean equality between the sexes. Gradually, it became identified with equality in the job market and eventually the conceptual field was extended to society more broadly so that, today, the conflict is about the equalisation of equality between the sexes with equality among ethnic minorities or between disabled and able-bodied people. Slowly, the concept of the politics of equality is taken over by politics of multiplicity. We are no longer able to define employment policies only in respect of equality between the sexes, but must also have regard to a flexibility and multiplicity that includes a variety of people: men, women, young people, old people, Muslims, Christians, weak people, strong people and so on. In this way, the concepts reach into the future: they define a space of signification and they define the meaning of the struggle for meaning.

Conclusion

The history of concepts thereby suggests an analytical strategy, which analyses history as a semantic struggle about turning words into concepts through the condensing a wide range of meaning into the concepts. Of course, this is not a linear history. A word can remain the same even though its meaning changes. A concept can remain the same even though its linguistic designation changes. A concept can survive even though its content changes and so on.

This raises a question that is parallel with (but probably not identical to) Laclau's question of hegemony and floating signifiers. According to Laclau, a hegemonic struggle can only take place if the structure is open – if the signifiers float above the signified – and the hegemonic struggle is therefore about arresting the floating. The concept of the floating signifier appears to function in a similar way to Koselleck's notion of concept. The ambiguity of the concept indicates that the concept does not possess a fixed relation to the fact to which it refers, in the same way that Koselleck's definition implies that the concept moves into the fact by adding meaning to it. Both characteristics of the concept (its floating and creative qualities) form the conditions for a semantic battle.

Semantic field analysis and counter-concepts

According to Koselleck, the analysis of the shaping, endurance and sociohistorical effects of individual concepts should happen in conjunction with an analysis of the way concepts appear in relation to other concepts – what he calls *semantic fields*. The analytical division of concept and field can simultaneously be seen as a distinction between diachronic and synchronous analytical strategies. Only through a continuous oscillation between the two perspectives "does the political and social process of change emerge" (Ifversen, 1997, p 451, author's translation).

Unfortunately, neither the definition of the semantic field nor the strategy for the analysis of semantic fields is sufficiently developed. Koselleck thematises the semantic field by means of the concept of '*counter-concepts*' in the article 'The historical–political semantics of asymmetric counter-concepts' (1985). Counter-concept is an analytical concept, which can be brought to bear on the relationships between concepts within a field. Counter-concept is defined by Koselleck as a concept that is in constitutive opposition to another, for example man/woman, public/secret, tolerance/intolerance. Any concept therefore obtains meaning from its counter-concept, and it is therefore crucial to study the shaping of concepts in relation to the shaping of counter-concepts.

It is not completely clear whether Koselleck believes that all conceptual relations contains the characteristics of concept/counter-concept or whether 'counter-concept' is one among many possible analytical concepts that can be used when analysing concepts within their semantic fields. Consequently, it is unclear whether Koselleck's article provides a general or specific example for the analyses of semantic fields. With this reservation in mind, the idea behind the analysis of counter-concepts is briefly outlined below.

Counter-concepts

Koselleck links the notion of counter-concept with the question of the construction of collective identities, in particular the construction of political subjects. He asserts that the construction of identities always involves *asymmetric classification* – identities are always shaped in asymmetric relations between 'us' and 'them'. The simple identification of the 'us' offers far from adequate conditions of giving 'us' the capacity to act:

> But a 'we' group can become a politically effective and active unity only through concepts which are more than just names or typifications. A political or social agency is first constituted through concepts by means of which it

circumscribes itself and hence excludes others; and therefore, by means of which it defines itself. A group may empirically develop on the basis of command or consent, of contract or propaganda, of necessity or kinship, and so forth; but however constituted, concepts are needed within which the group can recognize itself as a functioning agency. In the sense used here, a concept does not merely denote such an agency, it marks and creates the unity. The concept is not merely a sign for, but also a factor in, political or social groupings. (Koselleck, 1985, p 160)

Accordingly, political identities from movements, parties, interest groupings and so on are always constructed across the classification 'us'/'them', since there is no 'us' without 'them' and the exclusion of 'them' from 'us' is constituent for the identity of 'us'. It is important to emphasise the asymmetric character of the distinction in the same way that it is critical to realise that 'them' is not an ontological category. 'They' do not refer to an objective fact – in Lacanian terms, one could say that 'they' speak in 'us'.

Subsequently, concepts are necessary in order for a group to define and recognise itself as a functioning subject. Concepts not only classify but also mark and create unity. Again, it is important to bear in mind that concepts exist in a concentration of *ambiguous* meaning that ensues as a fundamental quality of the constitution of the group. Thus, the semantic struggle about concepts becomes central to the shaping of political identities.

In effect, this paves the way for studies of how political identities are shaped in conjunction with the designation of concepts and counter-concepts to specific identities: the construction of the bourgeois (as opposed to the proletarian), of the socialist (as opposed to the liberal), of the West (as opposed to the East), of the Protestant (as opposed to the Catholic). Moreover, it allows for studies of the effects that the shaping of concepts has on the possibilities for the shaping of identity. Often, a concept will prevail whereas its counter-concept will be replaced, so that, for example, the opposition of the West contra the East transforms into the West contra Communism, which changes again into the West contra the Muslim world.

Singularity/generality

Still, the creation of identity through counter-concepts cannot occur without tension in the relationship between, in Koselleck's terms, *singularity* and *generality*. In many ways, this separation coincides with Laclau's distinction between *particular* and *universal* (a point to which I return in Chapter Three). On the one hand, we can ascertain that concepts such as 'movement', 'party' and 'interest group' can be exercised on equal terms in the self-construction of a range of different identities. The concepts of 'movement', 'party' and 'interest group' are *transferable* in the sense that they can be subsumed, applied and transcribed by many different groups in a large number of contexts. Similarly, the identities that are constructed in association with the concepts of 'movement', 'party' and 'interest group' are *reciprocal*, in the sense that they do not exclude and incapacitate each other.

For example...

In the current Danish Parliament there are 10 parties that all shape their identities by referring to the concept of 'party', which, in itself, does not present a problem. The Social Democrats and *Venstre* (Liberal Party) are different, but reciprocal, identities that do not incapacitate each other.

On the other hand, Koselleck notes that there tends to be *singularisation*, that is, for the general to be subjected to the singular: "Historical agencies tend to establish their singularity by means of general concepts, claiming them as their own" (Koselleck, 1985, p 160). This is the case when a religious community lays claim to *the* Church, or when a political party claims to the represent *the* people. The Communist Party in the Soviet Union was an extreme example of the singularisation of the general designation of 'people' and 'party'. However, the same thing is true when generality is being restricted, for example through prohibiting certain political parties (such as the Communist Party or the National Socialist Party), or not allowing a religious community to be recognised as such. Generally, this applies whenever specific, that is, singular, requirements exist for affiliating oneself with the general. These requirements are always present, and hence the general is never truly general. There is always a limit to transferability, and reciprocal identities are therefore only reciprocal in relation to the identities they collectively exclude. The singular and the general never appear as pure differences, they always contaminate each other.

The problem of the singularisation of the general requires an analysis of how identities are constructed in relation to the shaping of concepts to focus always on how the tension between singularity and generality is defined.

For example...

When studying the formation of an organisation, however proper it may seem (and probably in particular when studying good organisations), we need to explore how this organisation singularises certain concepts. How, for one thing, is the concept of 'help' singularised as volunteer organisations subsume this concept in an increasing number of areas? For example, help provided by organisations such as Danchurchaid, Livsliniens and the Samaritans for suicidal people, patients' organisations and their counselling groups for people with cancer. How does 'help' increasingly become something that professional organisations induce and something, in effect, that is detached from the personal relationships of everyday living?

Furthermore, the question of singularisation impels the analyst to look at conceptual connections, because singularisation provokes counter-concepts from those groups that have been defined as the 'other'. Without awareness of how the origin of a concepts is constitutively related to its counter-concept, one loses sensibility to the sociohistorical effects of the shaping of concepts. Without the analysis of the semantic field, one ends up, as previously noted, in the barren history of words.

However, the counter-concept also possesses a history of its own. In other words, *the conditions of the shaping of counter-concepts change historically* and hence the conditions of the analysis of semantic fields also change by means of the opposition of concept/counter-concept. The tension between concept and counter-concept is not the same in a modern and a premodern context. Koselleck demonstrates this through an analysis of the conceptual history of counter-concepts and, in so doing, simultaneously analyses the conceptual–historical conditions of his own history of concepts!

Somewhat simplified, the history of counter-concepts is outlined below.

The history of counter-concepts

In antiquity, the opposition of the Hellenes and the barbarians demonstrates how counter-concepts can evolve. Until the 6th century BC, all non-Greeks were regarded as barbarians (those who spoke a strange language: 'bar-bar'). Subsequently, the barbarian became a counter-concept to the Hellenes. The Greeks began to describe themselves as Hellenes, and the notion of Hellenes versus barbarian became a universal structure that included all human beings in two groups. The structure was asymmetric, since the difference was always articulated by the Hellenes. The barbarian became symbolic of strangers, who were defined negatively and were attributed with qualities such as cowardice, brutality and ignorance. They were everything the Hellenes were not.

This distinction served different functions at different times. It was used to secure the unity of the Hellenes, to guard against civil war, as justification of the exploitation of the barbarians as slaves, and so forth. Initially, Hellenic and barbarian were mutually excluding concepts, in which the barbarians as strangers were demarcated in negative terms, but recognised as such. Later on, the concepts become territorialised so not only did they differentiate the stranger, they also demarcated the Hellenic territories from those of other countries.

Christianity introduced the next phase. Rather than maintaining the distinction between Hellenes and barbarians, Christians recruited members from both sides. They did not define themselves in opposition to Romans, Jews, Hellenes and so on; the concept 'Christian' was created potentially to encompass all human beings, regardless of race, class and so on. However, the distinction between Hellenic and barbarian was gradually superseded by the distinction between Christian and heathen, as a separation of religious and non-religious people. The distinction was construed temporarily, according to the prevailing notion that all heathens would eventually become Christians. This temporality installed a dynamics in Christianity. Gradually, however, through the crusades, for example, becoming a Christian was not just an option. Exclusion and expulsion became the other side of Christianity.

The third phase is represented by humanisation. Until this point, beginning with the renaisance, 'man' signified the unity of differences. Humankind was the sum of the Hellenes and the barbarians, and, later, the sum of the Christians and the heathens. Today, however, humankind and humanity have developed into an all-encompassing counter-concept that outdoes the opposition between Christians and heathens. This has happened in conjunction with the discovery of America and general globalisation, which means it is no longer possible to discover and annex new land ad infinitum; and the dispersal of the Christians into different religious communities, which means that the concept of 'Christian' in itself is no longer singular. Humanity thus emerges as a concept that produces a minimum definition uniting the divided Christians.

At the same time, we see a gradual repression by political theory of theology with God as the Creator. Humanity is generalised as a concept in relation to which all other concepts become particular. The generalised concept of humanity obtains a critical function – it serves as the foundation for the criticism of things as *in*human. As the all-encompassing concept of humanity is subsumed by the political, it attains totalitarian effects. Humanity changes side from being a counter-concept to becoming a concept, but this process turns it into an *empty category* that must constantly be imbued with new meaning. Accordingly, this necessitates an internal differentiation of humanity into superior and inferior people in an attempt to charge the empty category with meaning. At first, the difference superior/inferior person is transcribed from the societal hierarchy of superior/inferior differences, and refers the superior people to the leading classes of society. Then the distinction is liberated from the concepts of class and hierarchy. A superior person is no longer someone who belongs to a particular class, but someone who is 'more than human' and thus incarnates humanity as such. In the writings of Karl Marx, the relationship between superior and inferior people is reversed and, in effect, superiority becomes a concept laden with negativity, which functions as a critique of leading people who think too much of themselves. The rest of the history is well known.

Thus, not only do the definitions of concept and counter-concept change, the tension between them also changes. At first, the 'other' is defined negatively but recognised as such. Then the concepts become territorialised and grow to demarcate control of space. Subsequently, the relationship between concept and counter-concept is temporalised so that, in effect, people associated with the counter-concept can surpass the difference from counter-concept to concept. Finally, the concept is totalised and generalised, which turns it into an empty category that needs to be continually imbued with new meaning. It is therefore impossible to possess any preconceived knowledge of the precise characteristics of a counter-concept, which means that the construction of the analytical concepts becomes an integral part of the concept-historical analysis.

Five fundamental prelinguistic distinctions

As we have seen, Koselleck forms a distinction between the diachronic (in which studies of the rise, duration and transformation of the individual concepts are conducted) and the synchronous (which addresses the structural history of the extended lines, focusing on the construction and displacement of semantic fields). However, Koselleck actually employs yet another level, a metahistorical or *prelinguistic* level, which consists of *couples of opposition* or two-sided differences that precede the historical articulation of the concepts. They are differences or antitheses "without which no history can come to be, regardless of the forms they take on in particular cases – economic, religious, political, or social, or something involving all these empirical factors" (Koselleck, 1989, p 651). Evidently, all these prelinguistic couples of opposition are:

> grasped by man [sic] linguistically: by means of language they are reshaped socially or regulated politically. There is no acting human community that does not determine itself linguistically. It is almost always membership of a certain linguistic community that determines whether one is included or excluded. It is almost always the capacity to master certain modes of speech or specialized languages that decides whether one will move higher or lower, up or down, in a society. Almost always there are linguistic norms that are generation-specific and that sort out, diachronically, the experiences and hopes of the old from those of the young man, as a linguistic being, simply cannot avoid transforming the metahistorical givens linguistically in order to regulate and direct them, so far as he can. (Koselleck, 1989, p 652)

Koselleck's aim is to connect the history of concepts to Heidegger's existentialism, and the couples of opposition below are originally taken from Heidegger's *Being and time* (1978). Koselleck distinguishes between three prelinguistic couples of opposition, and my understanding is that these three couples form a sketch for later elaboration. The three couples are:

- before/after;
- inside/outside;
- up/down.

(They are sometimes portrayed as five couples: before/after; birth/death; inside/outside; friend/enemy; up/down.)

Before/after

Any history is, by its nature, poised between a before and an after, and this distinction is prelinguistic insofar as we are always living in the space between birth and death. This means not only that the lifespan is limited, but also that we live with death as the horizon and know that murder as well as suicide is possible. The distinction is furthermore prelinguistic in the sense that generations succeed generations, which results in a range of overlapping fields of experience that exclude each other in layers. Here, Koselleck speaks of diachronic conflicts (Koselleck, 1987, pp 11-14, 1989).

Koselleck extended the difference before/after in his distinction between *space of experience* and *horizon of expectation* (Koselleck, 1985, pp 226-88). 'Space of experience' and 'horizon of expectation' should be understood as epistemological categories. There can be no time–space relationship and thus no history without a conceptual formation of a space of experience and a horizon of expectation. The present does not exist in itself but only in the tension between a space of experience and a horizon of expectation, and all forms of political and social action must therefore ascribe to this tension. It is of great significance that it is a *couple* of opposition, that is, a two-sided difference: there is no experience without expectation and vice versa. The space of experience and the horizon of expectation thus corrupt one another; no side of the difference holds a preliminary status of privilege. The space of experience is seen as present past (that is, as the events that have been incorporated and remembered), while expectations designate present future (which directs itself towards the forthcoming, towards that which has not yet been experienced, towards that which will be prompted later). The horizon of experience is the line behind which new experience will emerge that cannot yet be seen (Koselleck, 1985, p 273).

To Koselleck, historical time is created, in continuously changing patterns and relations, by the mere tension between expectation and experience. Concept–historical analysis should uncover that which applies over time as expectation and experience, but also the tensions and relationships between expectation and experience, which are historical and must be exposed by the semantic analysis (Koselleck, 1985, p 275).

Inside/outside

No society or human action exists without a distinction between inside and outside. The distinction inside/outside is constitutive for the spaciousness of history:

> In this formal opposition, too, lie the seeds of varies potential histories.
> Whether it be the embattled retreat into a cave, or the forcible enclosure of
> a house, whether it be the drawing of a border that occasions, or concludes,
> a conflict, or rites of initiation, whether we are talking about grants of

asylum, or secret societies, or the examination systems and admissions qualifications that create modern social entities, or membership in a political community into which one normally is born – in all these cases the difference between 'inner' and 'outer' remains fundamental for the conflicts that arise and for their resolutions, fundamental, in short, for the histories with which we are all familiar. (Koselleck, 1989, p 651)

The distinction inside/outside is pushed to its extremes analogous to the friend/enemy distinction (at times, however, Koselleck completely separates the two distinctions). Inside we stand shoulder to shoulder in respect of our common welfare; outside is that which threatens our welfare:

> We have to understand that the couple of opposition of friend and enemy formally addresses mortality, which emerges behind the scene of all human self-organization. Regardless of whether in actual history Greeks and Barbarians or Greeks and Greeks fight each other, whether Christians and heathens have fought or Christians among themselves, whether the modern unities of action establish themselves in the name of humanity and treat the opponent as a brute, or the unities of action consider themselves subjects of class in order to actually overrule the classes – the empirical extension in its diachronic succession presupposes the couple of opposition of friend and enemy. (Koselleck, 1987, pp 14-15, author's translation)

Up/down

There are also different positions within a community. On the inside, we are joined against the things or people on the outside, but inside this community one can be up or down. The distinction between up and down can therefore define the internal pecking order. Nevertheless, the distinction can be articulated in countless ways, for example as a master/slave relationship, as in Greek and old-European terminology, or as the democratic political system of modern times that provides the standards for a continuous exchange of up/down positions (Koselleck, 1989, p 651). In politics, for example, the ruling party might be in opposition after the elections; new parties are established and voted into Parliament while other parties lose their support and dissolve. There can be no political self-organisation, no distribution of relationships of dependency and hence no history without the broadest definition of the distinction up/down.

Collectively, the three (or five) couples of opposition form the metahistorical conditions of the constitution of history: "According to Heidegger, we are dealing with existential definitions, that is, a particular kind of transcendental categories which indicate the possibility of histories without, however, describing specific histories" (Koselleck, 1987, p 20). In my opinion, Koselleck wishes to introduce three points.

45

First, he wants to install a distinction between *history* and *language*, which simultaneously inserts a distinction between *the occurrence* and *the articulation* of the occurrence as an event. Articulation, however, only becomes intelligible in relation to history. The distinction between history as a chain of occurrences and the articulation of these chains is itself constituent of the relationship between them:

> It is this difference between history in the actual process of its occurrence and history in its linguistic elaboration that remains, in any case, fundamental for their relationship. In any case, this difference between history as it takes place and its adaptation in language is constituent of the relationship between them. (Koselleck, 1989, p 652)

The same applies to the language that precedes the events and contributes, in spoken or written form, to triggering the events. Moreover, the articulation is a process of selection (my choice of words!). Not all occurrences become articulated as events and those that do become events could equally have been articulated as different events. Finally, some occurrences simply do not allow for articulation; language fails and takes the form of a boisterous silence:

> When the fluctuating distinction between 'inner' and 'outer' hardens into passionate conflict between friend and foe, when the inevitability of death is pre-empted by killing or by self-sacrifice, when the relation between 'above' and 'below' leads to enslavement and permanent subjugation or to exploitation and class struggle, or when the tension between the sexes leads to degradation – in all these cases there will occur events, or chains of events, or even cataracts of events, which are beyond the pale of language, and to which words, all sentences, all speech can only react. There are events for which words fail us, which leave us dumb, and to which, perhaps, we can only react with silence. (Koselleck, 1989, p 652)

Second, by employing the couples of opposition, Koselleck seeks to establish a space outside of language (although Koselleck is clearly aware that he has defined the five couples *within* language) that can define some fundamental guidelines for the history of concepts. This space outside language enables him to raise questions about how the five couples are active through history, how they are conceptualised over time, unfolded within different semantic fields and, in general, how, across the five distinctions, new semantic structures that constitute society and its players are continuously created.

Third, the metahistorical couples of opposition serve as a point of reflection for historiography, since historiography is subject to the same prelinguistic distinctions. Accordingly, Koselleck conducts a rather extensive critique of the historical-philological criticism:

- because it disregards the fact that historical reality only exists in shapes of language;

- because it disregards the fact that a selection of that which has been deemed worthy of reminiscence has already taken place;
- because it disregards that it is always the linguistically-fixed events that imbue unique events with their meaning of relative duration or specific signification;
- most importantly, because it fails to explain why formerly reliable and, for that reason, abandoned histories have to be rewritten at all (Koselleck, 1989, pp 661-6).

Conclusion

Koselleck's history of concepts consists of a combination of two analytics, between which one is continuously going back and forth. One is the diachronic analysis that focuses on single objects and their origins and transformation. These studies concern the shaping and consolidation of meaning into words, which are thereby transformed into objects that reach into the future by means of the constituent effect they have on, for example, the shaping of political agents, their identity and their ability to act. The study of the history of concepts is simultaneously a study of the semantic battle about concepts, including a battle about occupying concepts, about generalising concepts and about singularising the general.

On the other hand, synchronous analysis studies the way concepts always come into being in relation to other concepts in a semantic field. A semantic field is organised as the relationship between concepts and their counter-concepts. Prelinguistic couples of opposition provide guiding differences for the analysis of counter-concepts.

Koselleck's concept-historical analytical strategy is summarised in Figure 2.1.

Figure 2.1: Synchronous versus diachronic

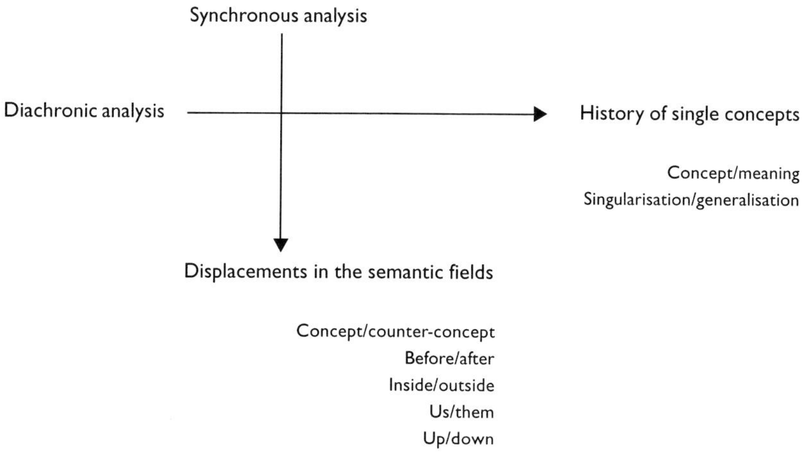

Synchronous analysis

Diachronic analysis ——————————————→ History of single concepts

Concept/meaning
Singularisation/generalisation

Displacements in the semantic fields

Concept/counter-concept
Before/after
Inside/outside
Us/them
Up/down

More schematically, the concept-historical analytical strategy is outlined in Table 2.1. The left-hand column indicates the analytical strategy; the centre column indicates the general inquiry of the analytical strategy; the right-hand column provides a concrete example of a possible conceptual history. The example used in this table is the abnormalisation of eating.

In Western Europe, we have no real lack of food. On the contrary, obesity seems to have been conceptualised as the most significant nutritional problem. However, if we take a closer look at the articulation of issues concerning food, the problem is not simply an excess of fat and the solution is not simply good nutritional information. Obesity appears to have been conceptualised, not only as a symptom of malnutrition, but as a signal of an unhealthy lifestyle. Nutritional experts no longer speak only of our food; they believe they are able to tell us how to live our lives. Nutritional policies have become life policies. Why is it that so many heterogeneous meanings – such as 'healthy living', 'nutriments', 'body-consciousness', 'prevention', 'assessments of lifestyle risks', 'individual responsibility' – have been condensed into our present concepts of eating? This is a typical concept-historical analysis.

Table 2.1: Koselleck's analytical strategies

Analytical strategy	General question	Example
Conceptual history	How is meaning condensed into concepts, thus constituting the space of possibility of the semantic battle?	How are 'healthy living', 'nutrients', 'body-consciousness', etc condensed into the concept of 'eating', thus constituting a conflict of life policies?
Semantic field analysis	How do concepts appear in relation to counter-concepts, thus creating a semantic field?	How does the concept of eating appear in relation to counter-concepts, thus creating a semantic field that pertains to nutritional policies?

The discourse theory of
Ernesto Laclau

The Argentinian Ernesto Laclau has conducted one of the most comprehensive rewritings of Foucault's discourse analysis. Ernesto Laclau currently works in the Department of Government, Essex University, UK; throughout his career he has been interested in questions of politics and the state. He was associated with the Marxist criticism of the 1970s and had a similar perspective to those of Louis Althusser and Antonius Gramsci. In 1985, he published the book *Hegemony and socialist strategy*, written together with Chantal Mouffe (1985). In this book, he formulates his final departure from Marxism and defines a new critical project, constructed around a discourse-analytical reconstruction of the concept of hegemony. With Chantal Mouffe, he conducts a genealogical analysis of the concept of hegemony and reaches an entirely new definition of the concept detached from the Marxist figures. At the same time, he reconstructs Foucault's discourse analysis in order to define a general, pure discourse analysis in which all the non-discursive elements found in Foucault's work have been removed. By defining the concept of hegemony as central to discourse theory, it is restored as a political theory. As far as I am aware, Ernesto Laclau is alone in defining discourse analysis as a political theory. I will return to this point later in this chapter.

Ernesto Laclau has maintained his political discourse theory since 1985. His work is exclusively theoretical and, to my knowledge, he has conducted no empirical discourse analyses, although he has performed certain deconstructions of concepts, which are of empirical importance (for example, the concept of representation; Laclau, 1993b). His theoretical work has primarily consisted of clarifying and systematising discourse theory; he has not, however, emphasised the development of analytical tools or operational strategies. Rather, his aim has always been a general, political discourse theory. In addition to numerous conceptual definitions, one can trace a certain shift in the central focus from discourse analysis towards deconstruction. Deconstruction has always clearly accompanied discourse theory but, at present, Ernesto Laclau writes more about deconstruction than about discourse analysis, without having left discourse analysis behind. Similarly, his current inspiration stems less from Foucault and Althusser, and increasingly from Derrida, Lacan and Zizek[1]. To a large extent it is possible to see in Laclau conceptual sets that refer back to each of these influences respectively. The concepts 'discourse', 'discourse analysis', 'moment', 'genealogy', 'articulation' and 'regulated dispersion' all derive from Foucault. Concepts such as 'floating signifier', 'empty signifier' and 'nodal point' derive from Lacan and Zizek. Finally, the concepts 'undecidability', 'deconstruction', 'logic of supplementation' and 'never fully closed structures' derive from Derrida.

This chapter presents selected key concepts and discusses the aim of Laclau's discourse analysis, including the particular relationship between deconstruction and discourse analysis that I believe suggests itself in Laclau.

Discourse

Let us begin with the concept of discourse. This, of course, is taken from Foucault, but in this context it embodies a more unambiguous and general definition. Laclau defines *discourse* as a structural totality of differences (Laclau and Mouffe, 1985, pp 105-14): "When, as a result of an articulatory practice, one has become capable of configuring a system of exact different locations, this system of different locations is called discourse" (Laclau, 1985, p 113).

Discourse, articulation, discoursivity

There are two important distinctions in respect to the further development of discourse theory in Laclau. These are different from the other theories presented in this book. The first distinction is between *articulation* and *discourse*, congruent with the relationship between practice and system. Articulation is designated by any practice that establishes relationships, that is, differences and similarities between elements (Laclau and Mouffe, 1985, p 105). Discourse is not in itself a practice but differs exactly by being the *result* of a practice, which, from the observing position of the discourse analyst, can be charged with the characteristics of an orderly pattern of differences. Contrary to Luhmann's notion of system, discourse as a system contains no *self* that is capable of differentiating itself from its surroundings. Hence, practice is not located in the separate discourses, although it exists in a discursive setting, without, however, having to admit the symmetrical character of the discourse.

This leads to the second distinction between *discoursivity* and *discourse*. Within this distinction, discoursivity signifies the fact that identities (objects, subjects, technologies, problems and so on) inevitably appear relationally, for example, only in relation to something else do social identities take on meaning. But these relationships do not necessarily possess the systemic character of discourse – the different locations of the identities can be imprecise and floating. Thus, the division between discoursivity and discourse is simultaneously a division between floating and fixed (or partially fixed) relationships. This brings us to the question of emergence, that is:

• How does a discourse emanate from and ascribe systemic properties to relationships?

Using the distinction between discoursivity and discourse, discourse can be observed as a never-completed fixation process that takes place through articulation within a field of discoursivity with drifting relations: "Any discourse is constituted as an attempt to dominate the field of discoursivity, to arrest the flow of differences, to construct a centre" (Laclau and Mouffe, 1985, p 112).

This also means that the relationship between articulation and discourse is a dynamic one. The ever-floating and hence undecided structure of discourse prompts articulation as that which attempts to arrest the flow of differences and determine the undetermined without, however, being able to conclusively do so. Consequently, articulation can never be presupposed based on discourse. Articulation is more than, and must be more than, the realisation of the structure.

Discursive (nodal) points

The centre of the discourse, striving to arrest the flow of relations without ever becoming a centre, consists of privileged discursive points. As Derrida has shown and as Laclau maintains, a centre must, in order to be a centre in the classical sense, exist simultaneously within and without the system whose relationships are being fixed by the centre. However, since the centre of the discourse itself is defined discursively (that is, defined within), the centre can never be present outside the system of differences, extending the discursive game infinitely (Derrida, 1976). More simply: there is no place outside the discourse that can remain untouched by it and is able to define its order. As a result, the discursive battle is capable of constantly making the centre pivotal to that battle in such a way that it changes the rules of the discursive game. Hence no differences are fixed; at most they can obtain partial fixation. Laclau identifies these centres that never quite become centres as *nodal points* (which is a translation from Lacan of the French *point de capition*). The relationship between articulation, discoursivity, discourse and nodal points is summarised thus:

> The practice of articulation, therefore, consists in the construction of nodal points which partially fix meaning; and the partial character of this fixation proceeds from the openness of the social, a result, in its turn, of the constant overflowing of every discourse to the infinitude of the field of discoursivity. (Laclau and Mouffe, 1985, p 113)

The floating surplus of meaning and undecidability

As already noted, Laclau's point of departure is a definition of discourse as a structure, but he stresses on several occasions that the structure never reaches full closure. On the contrary, a structure tends to collapse from within because it is never able to completely fix its elements into steady relationships, because it cannot irrefutably locate something outside the structure to define and maintain itself.

This is a central point and one that extends to all parts of discourse theory. The necessary incompleteness of the structure is, regardless of the specific focus or perspective, a recurrent theme throughout discourse theory, and, depending on the perspective, the problem is given different definitions. It is therefore necessary to further elaborate this point.

The political

The first detail pertains to the *political*. Politics happen precisely because structures are never complete. If a structure were able to reach full closure, it would exclude the political. Because of the eternal undecidability of the discursive structures, however, politics acquire a central role within all structures as that moment when undecidable structures, demanding a conclusion or closure, become partially fixed. Discourse analysis is a political analysis of the way contingent relations become fixed in one way, but could have been fixed in many others.

S/subjects

Furthermore, this is the most substantial critique of Althusser's ideology theory. In Althusser, there is no room for the political because the structures are seen as complete. This is illustrated by the *problem of the subject*. Althusser makes a distinction between the small subject and the big Subject. The big Subject is the model for the creation of all smaller subjects. When an individual or collective is defined as subject it is granted a steady position in relation to the big Subject (or the master subject); a steady position in the structure of the ideology. The individual becomes subject to the Court, to God, to the Economy, or whatever the big Subject happens to be in the proclaiming ideology in question. In relation to the declaration, the individual faces a simple choice between reason and madness, between accepting her/his place and becoming a 'sensible' subject, or being excluded from reason without the possibility of defining oneself as a subject outside the ideology. If, on the other hand, the structure is seen as incomplete, the need for politics emerges. The individual cannot fully identify with the subject position provided by the discourse but is forced into filling in the structural gaps through identification, and this identification process is precisely political because it requires a choice that cannot be explained away – a choice about the subject's self-constitution.

Signs and signifiers

Moreover, the question of the structure's incompleteness appears in relation to the notion of signs. The point of departure is de Saussure's concept of signs (1990). A sign in this context consists of the unity of the difference between signifier and signified, between, for example, a sound-image and the concept to which the sound-image refers (for example, c-a-t/cat). For de Saussure, it is the relationship between the signs that constitute the meaning of the sign (for example between the signs c-a-t/cat, d-o-g/dog, h-o-u-s-e/house, d-o-g-l-e-a-s-h/dog leash). Language exists as the system of relations between signs, and language is perceived of as a complete system of fixed relations. But what happens if that structure is seen as incomplete? That would mean that signifiers and their signified were not irrefutably tied to each other. Instead they would be partially free floating layers on top of each other; the signifiers would be floating signifiers.

The expression 'floating signifier' was first used by Claude Lévi-Strauss, although it was the psychoanalyst Jaques Lacan who unfolded the concept theoretically (Macey, 1988, p 137; Lacan, 2001, pp 146-78). Lacan demonstrates how the sliding of the signifier across the signified forces the signifier to step into, or down onto, the level of the signified. Hence, the signifiers influence that which they signify. This means that signifiers receive a particular status in relation to signification and to the signified.

For example...

Lacan's favourite example is that of two identical doors next to each other. The doors (the signified) are not signified in the same way, however – one door is signified 'Gentlemen' and the other door is signified 'Ladies'. The effect is obvious: the exchange of signifiers cuts through the bar (/) and into the signified. The incomplete structure thus appears, not only in the sliding relationships between the signs, but also insofar as the bar that separates signifier from signified proves to be less watertight than assumed by de Saussure.

Laclau transfers these concepts to discourse analysis, which focuses on:

- how signifiers and the signified do not relate to each other in a predetermined relationship;
- how discursive signification happens precisely in relation to displacements in the signification of the signified;
- how which signifier is fixed above a given signified is very much a political issue.

The discursive battle is therefore a conflict or struggle over which signifiers are to be tied to which signified.

For example...

A dead seal lands on the beach. How should we signify this event? There are still seals off the shore of xville; pollution takes new victims; the ruthless over-fishing of herring is starving the seal population; or another flu epidemic ravages the seals off the sound? The signifier steps down into the signified and transforms the seal (the signified) into a signifier of its own – the dead seal signifies the diversity of nature, pollution, a flu epidemic, and so on. The signifier is also obviously political: should we take measures against fishing or pollution, or simply wonder about the whim of nature?

This battle over fixing sliding signifiers is, as I have noted before, a battle over the definition of nodal points (or, to use Lacan's term, *privileged signifiers*), which can arrest the sliding of the many signifiers across the signified.

Besides the application of these concepts, Laclau introduces yet another concept – the notion of the *empty signifier*. (I believe this is Laclau's invention, although, here too, he is heavily indebted to Lacan.) The question of the signifier that signifies nothing emerges in Lacan's famous article on the non-existence of *the* woman: "This *the* is a signifier characterized by being the only signifier which cannot signify anything" (Lacan, 1982, p 144). Such a signifier is the only signifier capable of ending and defining a limit for the chain of signification. The analogue question in Laclau addresses the partial finality of the discursive game. The empty signifier is used to signify that which does not allow for signification, that is, the limit of the discursive signification: "An empty signifier can consequently only emerge if there is a structural impossibility in signification as such, and only if this impossibility can signify itself as an interruption of the structure of sign" (Laclau, 1996a, p 37).

Summary

A discourse consists of different elements of signification, which only obtain identity through their mutual differences in the discourse. The condition of mutual differences, however, is that the elements are identical or equivalent in respect to belonging to the discourse and existing within the boundaries of the discourse. On other words, on the one hand, elements can only form an identity through their mutual differences, while on the other hand, the differences are cancelled out by the equivalent relation provided by the elements' attachment to the discursive structure. This is only possible if there are different types of differences; if a difference exists that is radically constituent for the differences of the system. Laclau identifies this difference as the *excluding boundary*. Within the boundary exists a system of relational elements; outside the boundary exists only pure, indifferent being in relation to which every element of the system is equally different. Thus, outside the boundary only radical indifference exists (which is why the distinction inside/outside the system should not be confused with Luhmann's distinction between surroundings/system).

The empty signifier occurs, in effect, as a possibility for the signification of "the pure cancellation of all difference" (Laclau, 1996a, p 38). Laclau summarises the argument thus:

> There can be empty signifiers within the field of signification because any system of signification is structured around an empty place resulting from the impossibility of producing an object which, nonetheless, is required to be the systematicity of the system. (Laclau, 1996a, p 40)

An empty signifier is that which signifies the indifferent and the cancellation of difference. All differences must be *equally* different in relation to it, while also being different from each other. Locating and analysing the empty signifier entails a signification of the ultimate limit of the discourse but, since such a signifier will always be inside the discourse, it will never be possible to represent it fully.

Laclau illustrates the relationship between equivalence and difference as portrayed in Figure 3.1.

Hegemonic analysis and the battle of fixating

The formulation of the problem of floating elements of signification opens up a redefinition of the question of hegemony or supremacy in society. The concept of hegemony in Laclau's discourse theory functions, in short, by focusing the aim of discourse analysis. It is not the main purpose of discourse analysis to produce individual analyses of conceptual displacement or individual battles over the fixating of signifiers, but rather to uncover the general hegemonic relationships in society, and conditions for the transformation of hegemony.

With the discourse-analytical reconstruction of the concept of hegemony, other traditionally Marxist concepts find new formulations as well, including, first and foremost, the concepts 'opposition' and 'antagonism'. However, first, we will only indicate the direction of the conceptual turn.

The notion of hegemony is linked directly to the argument about the incompleteness of structures and to the continually fully or partially floating elements of discourse. The basic understanding is that hegemony is only possible when something exists that can be hegemonised, and that this is only the case when discourse lacks final fixation, when the discursive elements hold a surplus of meaning and when the signifiers are not irreversibly linked to the signified. Consequently, hegemony signifies the never-concluded attempts to produce a fixation, to which there will always be a threat. As Laclau metaphorically notes, hegemony "is like writing in water. It is something impossible, unstable, and vulnerable, but to a certain extent still something

Figure 3.1: Chains of difference and equivalence

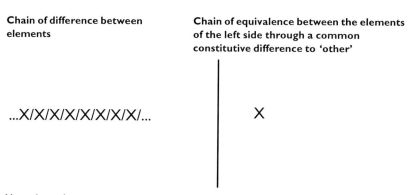

Chain of difference between elements	Chain of equivalence between the elements of the left side through a common constitutive difference to 'other'
...X/X/X/X/X/X/X/...	X

X equals an element

that can be accomplished" (Laclau, 1985, p 107). Hegemony creates the space for "a politics of signifiers" (Laclau, 1983).

Hegemonisation subsequently consists in the imposition onto elements of a certain way of relating to each other. This also means that hegemonisation brings elements together that have not previously been brought together (Laclau and Mouffe, 1985, pp 134-45). The economic hegemonisation in society appears in elements that were not earlier considered socioeconomic being suddenly recognised as such, and, furthermore, in these elements now relating to themselves as social economy. One example could be the emergence of policies for older people from the mid-1980s.

For example...

Until the mid-1980s the elements of residential homes, older people, home care, and older people's housing in Denmark were not associated with elements such as social–economic balance, inflation, finance and so on. From the mid-1980s, however, policies for older people became a central socioeconomic and political issue. Subsequently, a number of policy works are commissioned. This results in two things. First, residential homes, older people's housing, home care and other issues are brought together under the same policy umbrella through the joint formulation of policies for older people (which has never happened before). Second, policies for older people establish themselves through the formulation of a political expenditure issue about the social–economic coordination of public services for older people. Hence, the hegemonisation of policies for older people within the socioeconomic conception appears not as a hierarchy of relations of superiority and inferiority, but as the investment of a particular logic in the construction and shaping of policies for older people.

Discourse *analysis* versus deconstruction

As highlighted in the introduction to this chapter, there appears to be a traceable shift of focus in Laclau's writings, from discourse analysis to deconstruction. In this section, I will argue that discourse analysis and deconstruction provide two completely different perspectives, but that Laclau brings them into a complementary relationship in which the output of one becomes the input of the other. The bridge between them appears as that which Laclau calls 'logics'.

Discourse analysis is, as already noted, an analysis of the discursive system of dispersion – of the way discursive elements are dispersed and placed in relation to each other. Deconstruction is in no way synonymous with discourse analysis. Neither is it one 'technique' among several techniques within discourse analysis, but is in fact in clear opposition to discourse analysis.

Origins and definition of deconstruction

The concept of deconstruction derives from Derrida. In the article 'Letter to a Japanese friend' (Derrida, 1988), Derrida replies to a letter he has received in which he is asked the question: what, really, *is* deconstruction? Derrida, however, refuses to answer the question on the assumption that deconstruction in itself should be *anything* definite. Instead, Derrida chooses to elaborate on what deconstruction *ought not* to be, and in relation to discourse analysis the answer is rather interesting. Derrida emphasises that deconstruction is neither analysis nor criticism (Derrida, 1988): deconstruction is not analysis because it refuses to be reduced to simple principles and it is not criticism because there exists no place from which criticism can be conducted. Conversely, discourse analysis is precisely analysis because discourse analysis reduces and refers the many articulations to a particular system of dispersion. Even though discourse analysis does not claim, as does structuralism, to be able to refer to one simple principle but rather maintains the structural openness, the act of conducting a discourse analysis still requires a reductive description. I will leave whether or not discourse analysis is a form of criticism open to discussion. But I am of the definite opinion that deconstruction cannot be incorporated in a discourse analysis.

But then what *is* deconstruction? Derrida gives the answer to that question in a subordinate clause:"'deconstruction' is precisely the delimiting of ontology" (Derrida, 1988, p 4). But, since deconstruction consists of such 'delimiting', Derrida must also insist that deconstruction cannot be reduced in this way since it would then stand outside itself. The result is thus:"What deconstruction is not? Everything of course! What is deconstruction? Nothing of course!" (Derrida, 1988, p 5).

Naturally, this is a completely satisfactory definition, so I will endeavour to answer the question even if Derrida refuses to. My understanding of it is that deconstruction is about showing how differences are contingent, that is, deconstruction is about retracting or deconstructing differences by showing that they are not differences at all; that the 'bar' between two elements, which isolates one from the other, cannot be maintained. Even after the difference has been established, it is still contingent what it consists in, if at all. It is not a question of locating differences within a system, or a discourse, but a question of addressing the individual difference in order to prove that it is not valid. One example of this is the difference between speech and writing, which Derrida deconstructs in *Of grammatology* (1980). Here the issue is the dissolution of the difference between speech and writing, first by showing that writing precedes speech and second by posing the argument that speech and writing are both writing – one phonetic, the other graphic.

Deconstructing difference

The deconstruction of a difference does not end, however, once it has been shown that the difference is not valid. The illustration of the non-difference of the difference (so to speak) is simultaneously an illustration of those mechanisms or games that are present in each differentiation. The point is to see the difference as a mechanism in a game of signification. Usually, there appears to be a hierarchical relationship between the two elements in a difference – one tries to subjugate the other. By deconstructing differences, the relationship is usually reversed in such a way that what appears to be the norm is recognised as a game of dominance. This could, for instance, pertain to the concept of sign, which I have previously mentioned in this chapter. It would appear obvious to assume that the signified would hold the dominant side in the relation between signifier and signified. Without something to refer to, how can there be reference? But the deconstruction of the sign puts holes in the bar dividing the signifier from the signified and the signifier appears on the same level as the signified. Subsequently, the hierarchy of difference is reversed – the signifier becomes the dominant element and suddenly our attention is drawn to a central mechanism of signification. This type of mechanism is often referred to by Laclau as 'logic', and we are thus able to talk about a logic of signification as the mechanism present in signification and in the displacement of signification onto the signified.

The relationship between deconstruction and discourse analysis

Deconstruction cannot be incorporated into discourse analysis, but what, then, is the relationship between them when Laclau insists on using both. The answer is that the relationship is circular (see Figure 3.2). Deconstruction pinpoints mechanisms or logics whose unfolding within the discursive battles of history can be studied in discourse analysis. Discourse analysis, in return, is able to provide deconstruction with politically central concepts and dualities (two-sided differences) and so on. The logic of signification functions as a point of departure for a discourse analysis of, for example, the ecological discourse. What we examine here is the battle over how floating signifiers are to be fixed above the signified. We examine how names are interchanged; how some signifiers are sought out as privileged in order for them partially to fixate other signifiers (for example, nitrate pollution of drinking water); and finally, whether there is a breakdown in the signification logic in the form, for example, of an empty signifier, which causes all meaning to implode. This could focus on the notion of 'the ecological latitude'.

Figure 3.2: The relationship between deconstruction and discourse analysis

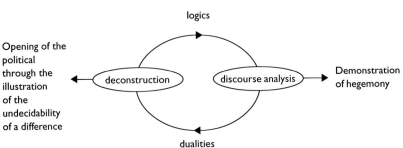

Logics therefore become clues or points of reference for discourse analyses. Discourse analysis analyses the hegemonic constellations within which logics play themselves out. Without logics as deconstructive input, discourse analysis could not obtain the same sensitivity in relation to the central mechanisms or to structural incompleteness. Laclau describes it thus:

> Deconstruction and hegemony are the two essential dimensions of a single theoretico-practical operation. Hegemony requires deconstruction: without the radical structural undecidability that the deconstructive intervention brings about, many strata of social relations appear as essentially linked by necessary logics and there would be nothing to hegemonise. But deconstruction also requires hegemony, that is, a theory of the decision taken in an undecidable terrain: without a theory of decision, that distance between structural undecidability and actuality would remain untheorised. (Laclau, 1996b, 59-60)

Logics

In recent years Laclau has conducted a number of deconstructions of different important political conceptual couples. Some of the logics that result from these are described below.

Logic of signification

We have already touched on the *logic of signification*. It is important to note that a number of Laclau's deconstructions in relation to the logics discussed below are simply applications of the logic of signification on the relationships of specific signifiers to their specific signified. Therefore, once one has a better understanding of the logic of signification, it is possible to explore much further.

Logic of representation

The designation of the *logic of representation* happens as a result of a deconstruction of the difference representative/represented (Laclau, 1993b). It is an assumption of prevailing political theory that the represented side of the difference is the dominant side. Representation only makes sense if it actually represents something. Furthermore, prevailing political theory discusses how representation can be distorted in relation to what it represents, which leads to a democracy-theoretical discussion about which institutions ensure the most accurate representation. Deconstruction leads to a reversal of the difference and to a displacement of the theoretical question of representation. Not only does the representative distort the represented, it also indispensably partakes in constructing the represented and can therefore never stay neutral in relation to it: "The relation representative–represented has to be privileged as the very condition of a democratic participation and mobilization" (Laclau, 1996b, p 49). This opens up the question of how the struggle of representation is always a struggle over the construction of the represented.

Logic of tolerance

The *logic of tolerance* indicates the mechanism that is present in the difference tolerance/intolerance. Here, too, the difference is reversed through deconstruction which shows that tolerance cannot be explained in itself without turning into its opposite. Consequently, intolerance is simultaneously the condition of the possibility and the impossibility of tolerance; the undecidability of the distinction extends the possibility of both poles. With the logic of tolerance we are able to study the hegemonic battle over what should be tolerated and what should not be tolerated (Laclau, 1996b, pp 50-2).

Logic of power

The *logic of power* indicates the mechanism present in the difference power/liberation. Once again, the difference is reversed. Jurisprudence assumes that freedom is the condition of power; power is the restriction of freedom and therefore earns its potential through freedom. Laclau reverses the difference and points out that what restricts freedom is also what makes it possible – a society free from power is an impossibility. Once again, this provides the basis for a discourse-analytical study of the continued negotiation and displacement of the power/freedom boundary (Laclau, 1993b, 1996b, pp 52-3).

Logic of equivalence; logic of difference

Moreover, Laclau configures what he calls logic of equivalence and logic of difference. It is not clear whether these logics are used in the same way as in the above examples. If so, they could be understood thus. Laclau chooses as his point of departure a deconstruction of the very difference difference/equivalence in order to show how differentiation holds implications in relation to the articulation of equivalence and, conversely, how, at the same time, equivalence affects differentiation. The two logics are central in Laclau's discourse analysis.

The logic of equivalence is the logic of simplification of the political sphere. Through the articulation of equivalence between elements, the possibility of an interchangeability of elements is increased. At the same time, the number of subject positions is reduced. For example, by making almost everything equivalent to social economy – from tax issues and the environment to equality – more and more elements can be included and interchanged within the same chain of values. Meanwhile, the number of positions through which one is able to participate in the conflict over taxes, the environment and equality is reduced.

Conversely, the logic of difference signifies the logic through which the political sphere is widened and increases its internal complexity. The elements do not become particularly interchangeable, but the number of subject positions (that is, the positions from which one can be political) is increased (Laclau and Mouffe, 1985, p 130).

Logic of universalisation

Finally, I wish to mention the *logic of universalisation*, which is based on the deconstruction of the difference particular/universal (Laclau, 1996b, p 59). Precisely because the universal is universal it ought to be able to stand alone. Deconstruction shows, however, that this is not possible: "The conclusion seems to be that the universality is incommensurable with any particularity yet cannot exist apart from the particular" (Laclau, 1992, p 90). This forms the basis for studies of how attempts are made to universalise the particular, and how universalisation defines what can be articulated as particular.

Conclusion

Laclau also configures a few other logics that are usually presented as aspects of almost all logics, including the *logic of supplement* and the *logic of impossibility*. The concept of logic does not therefore appear to be exercised completely consistently. The logic of supplement and the logic of impossibility involve a *meta*logic that might also apply to the logic of difference and the logic equivalence, but not to the logic of representation, which, one must assume, is bound by a particular historicity. We can therefore observe a division of duties between deconstruction and discourse analysis, but also a lack of theorisation of their mutual relationships, which appears as an inconsequent and insufficiently defined concept of logic. This raises a number of questions, particularly about universality:

- Are some logics more universal than others?
- And if they are not universal, what is their field of validity?
- What is the relationship between history and logic?
- What is the theory behind the definition of the central dualities in deconstruction?
- Is there a hierarchy of logics with, for example, the logic of universality being the most universal?
- If so, can the hierarchy of logics itself be deconstructed?

However, these questions do not change the fact that, analytically, the linking of deconstruction and discourse analysis is exceedingly powerful.

Conclusion

Laclau's two analytical strategies and the way they pose questions have been summarised in Table 3.1. In the right-hand column I have attempted to provide an example of a possible concrete analysis. The example used in this table is the issue of animal ethics that has taken place in most EU countries, in particular in the UK. A deconstructive analysis could address the discursive infinity of the debate about animal ethics. Ethics always claims to be universal, to be unavoidable, and to not let itself be deflected by pragmatic and specific circumstances. Ethics are only ethics if they raise themselves above concrete circumstances. A deconstructive analytical strategy, therefore, could address the duality of universal/particular in order to demonstrate that any claim for universality is always particular, and that the two sides of the duality must incessantly pollute and contaminate one another. Deconstruction could point to the conditions of impossibility of animal ethics. Subsequently, a hegemonic analysis would be able to analyse how the conditions of impossibility of ethics are unfolded in specific discursive battles about trying nevertheless to fixate animal ethics. Hegemonic analysis could point out different discursive attempts to fixate and how different attempts must exclude something from their discoursing in order to form a coherent discourse. The more militant discourses define production and financial prioritising as antagonistic opposites to ethics. These discourses would not be able to maintain their strong sense of unity without rejecting any kind of pragmatism, which, in turn, prevents them from ever gaining any form of hegemony. By contrast, production and economically oriented discourses of agriculture might involve ethics, but on behalf of the purity of ethics as precisely universal ethics. Ethics become temporalised. It is something that should be achieved in the long term and a consideration that, because of its temporal distance, must be weighed against other considerations in the present, such as the economy and production.

Table 3.1: Laclau's analytical strategies

Analytical strategy	General question	Example
Deconstruction	Which infinite logic is installed with a specific duality?	In what way does any discourse about animal ethics rely on the duality of universal/particular? Which infinite logic does any animal ethics therefore have to unfold?
Hegemonic analysis	How are discourses established through never-concluded battles about the fixation of floating elements of signification?	In what way is the signifier 'animal ethics' sought, given value and fixated in conflicts between different discourses with different strategies of equivalency and difference?

Note
[1] In the article 'Discourse', Laclau even distinguishes between two fundamental notions of discourse analysis – his own poststructuralist discourse analysis and Foucault's second-order phenomenology (Laclau, 1993b).

4

Niklas Luhmann's systems theory

Of the writers included in this book, Niklas Luhmann is unquestionably, and in many ways, the most comprehensive. He has written more than 50 books and over 400 articles. One of his goals has been to test the general stating power of systems theory by writing at least one book about each of the function systems of modern society. Hence, he has conducted extensive historical analyses of the scientific system, the political system, the system of arts, the educational system, the system of justice, the system of regions, love and family as a system, the system of mass media, and the system of economics. But his work is also the most comprehensive in another respect. Of the authors in this volume, Luhmann's work probably involves the highest number of different theoretical questions, provides the widest scope of theoretical approaches and possesses the highest degree of flexibility for the elaboration of projects within theory. However, in this book, we are not concerned with the many analyses of different social systems but only with the Luhmanian 'eye' for social systems as communication.

Luhmann's path towards the 'communication-theoretical turn' is completely different from that of Laclau and Foucault. The communication-theoretical turn did not appear until around 1980. Prior to this, Luhmann had suggested that meaning was the fundamental concept of sociology (Luhmann, 1990b, pp 21-79), but it was not until the beginning of the 1980s that he changed his notion of social systems as systems of action to an understanding of these systems as autopoietic systems of communication, consisting in and by communication. To a certain extent, Luhmann's systems theory can be viewed as a communication-theoretical rewriting of the systems theory of Talcot Parsons. In Parsons' work, the communication-theoretical inspiration stems not from French structuralism, but from a unique patchwork of the calculus of form from the mathematician Spencer-Brown, the theory of life as a system of autopoiesis from the biologist Maturana, the theory of information as differences that make a difference from the autodidact Bateson, and the theory of meaning from the phenomenologist Husserl.

Luhmann's theoretical architecture has often been compared to a labyrinth. This is not only because it is difficult to get in and even more difficult to get out, but particularly because it is not construed deductively. It is inductive in a very particular way and always allows for the observer to step back and ask: 'Why this particular concept?', through which all concepts suddenly appear in a new light. I will return to this point later in this chapter.

As there are so many different points of entry to the theory, it is by no means a given how to introduce Luhmann – there is no obvious first concept. Moreover, it appears that the concepts change 'colour' depending on the concept one chooses to begin with. Already, there are several conceptual dictionaries of Luhmann's systems theory (for example, Krause, 1996), one of which suggests specific routes and specific chronologies, by which one can approach Luhmann's concepts. In one sense, each route establishes its own systems theory. Here, I have chosen to begin with the concept of observation, which means that I prioritise the Spencer-Brownian Luhmann. Two alternatives are the Parsonian Luhmann (where the relation of system/evolution is central) and the Maturanian Luhmann (where the central concept is that of autopoiesis).

Systems theory as second-order observation

By choosing to define the concept of observation as a starting point, systems theory is thus defined as a theory about second-order observation. The concept of observation immediately doubles as, on the one hand, a general concept of observation and, on the other hand, as concrete and specific observations, which we, as systems theorists, can observe as observations precisely by means of a general concept of observation.

Form and difference

Luhmann's theory of observation is founded on a particular definition of form and difference, particularly inspired by Spencer-Brown (1969), von Foerster (1981) and Günther (1976). The basic premise is to view observations as *operations* that do not refer to conscious subjects but to differences. Luhmann simply defines observation as a specific operation of creating distinctions: *to observe is to indicate something within the boundaries of a distinction.* In the words of Spencer-Brown: "We take as given the idea of distinction and the idea of indication, and that we cannot make an indication without drawing a distinction" (Spencer-Brown, 1969, p 1).

For example...

We might, for example, fasten upon something artistic. 'Art' is then indicated. But art can only be indicated within the boundaries of a distinction. The opposite side could be ugliness, unsightliness, disharmony and so on, and this other side of the distinction makes a difference to the way art appears as an object to the observer. Therefore, what we observe is above all dependent on the distinction that defines the framework for what is indicated in the world at large.

Spencer-Brown indicates the difference as shown in Figure 4.1.

Figure 4.1:The sign of difference

Indication/distinction

Like anything else, the concept of observation must be grounded in a distinction. In Luhmann, it is the distinction indication/distinction. More precisely: observation is the unity of the distinction indication/distinction. To demarcate is to indicate or even name something in the world and, as previously noted, that demarcation always takes place as an indication of one side of a distinction. In Luhmann's universe, distinctions are always two-sided. A distinction possesses an inner side as well as an outer side; the inner side being the indicated side. The inner side is designated 'the marked space', while the outer side is designated 'the unmarked space'. Whenever there is observation, one side in the difference is marked and the other remains unmarked.

Such a distinction isolates the marked from the unmarked and it is therefore only possible for one side of the distinction to be indicated at a time. If both sides are marked, the distinction is cancelled out. It is not possible simultaneously to observe an object as beautiful and ugly – except over time – but then it is no longer the same observation. Hence, distinctions are always asymmetrical because only one side is marked (see Figure 4.2).

Through the observation of something, the blind spot of observation is shaped. The blind spot is the unity of the distinction that constitutes the framework for the observation. In Luhmann's theory, the unity of the distinction is defined as form. The blind spot of observation exists because of the fact that observation cannot see that it cannot see that which it cannot see.

Figure 4.2:The marked difference

m

Second-order observations

We are now closing in on systems theory. Luhmann attempts to establish his systems theory precisely as second-order observation. If first-order observation is the indication of something within a distinction, second-order observation is observation directed at first-order observation and its blind spot. Systems theory thus inquires about the blind spots of society and of the systems of society, about the distinctions that fundamentally decide what can appear in society and how.

Obviously, all second-order observations are also, at the same time, first-order observations, since they indicate first-order observation within a distinction. There exists, therefore, no privileged position for observation. This is illustrated in Figure 4.3.

Figure 4.3: A difference observed through a difference

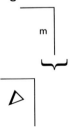

Reference

An observation does not merely indicate within a distinction. The operation of observation furthermore establishes a distinction between *self-reference* and *external reference*, between what is observed and the observing system. The observing system *comes into being* through observation, together with what is observed. The system does not precede the world it observes: both are constructed through the observation that separates them. The system is thus not constituent of the observation. On the contrary, it is the observation and the distinction actualised by it that decides how the world appears to which system. In this sense, reality is always systems relative and the operation of observation divides the world into system and environment. Thus, systems theory is based on three distinctions: indication/distinction, system/environment and first-/second-order observation.

First- and second-order observations

Let me clarify the conditions of first- and second-order observations. First-order observation is the observation by a system of something in the environment. First-order observations thus use external reference: they refer to the environment. Second-order observations, however, are observations of the observing system itself – not in any way but precisely as observer. Second-order observations are thus self-referential.

Distinctions

Observations of the first as well as the second order are observations within a distinction, but not all ways of distinguishing allow for second-order observation. Luhmann distinguishes between three ways of making a distinction:

- First, by distinguishing something from something else without specifying the other side of the distinction (for example, horse/not horse). What occurs in this distinguishing operation Luhmann simply refers to as *object* (Luhmann, 1993a, p 15).
- Second, by indicating in a way that restricts the other side of the distinction (for example, plus/minus, man/woman, warm/cold, Danish/foreigner). This type of distinction is referred to as *concept* and always implies a counter-concept (Luhmann, 1993a, p 16).
- Third, a particular variant of concepts, in which distinctions are made by copying a conceptual distinction and re-entering it into the inside or outside of the concept itself, to thereby indicate certain aspects of the concept. These are therefore concepts capable of conceptualising themselves. Such concepts are referred to by Luhmann as *second-order concepts*. Concepts of the second order are thus restrictive distinctions, which can be re-entered into or re-enter themselves. For example, the distinction of government/opposition can be re-entered into itself in the sense that both government and opposition are able to conceive of itself as having a government (a deciding fraction) and an opposition (an opposing minority).

A system is only able to observe itself if it indicates itself within the framework of a second-order concept. If a system is to observe itself as observer, the system is required to divide itself in two: the observer and the observed. Hence, Luhmann proposes that a system, constituted as the unity of the distinction system/environment, is only able to observe itself as observer if it can copy its guiding distinction and re-enter it into itself, that is, its ability to divide itself by entering the distinction system/environment into the system itself (Luhmann, 1995a, pp 37-55). This process of re-entry is illustrated in Figure 4.4.

Figure 4.4: The distinction system/environment re-entered as a part of itself

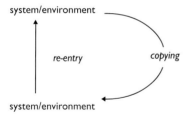

system/environment

re-entry   *copying*

system/environment

In the mathematical tradition following Spencer-Brown, such re-entry is indicated as shown in Figure 4.5.

Figure 4.5: The sign of re-entry

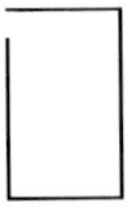

Source: Kaufmann, 1987, pp 53-72

Paradox

This way of thinking has a number of implications. On the level of first-order observation, observations are paradoxical, since the observer must distinguish without being able to choose her distinction. An observer of the first order cannot see the distinction on which her observation is based, and yet she can make distinctions. That is a paradox. Conversely, the observer of the second order sees that the observing observer can only see that which his distinction lets him see. He is thus able to see how the first-order paradox is removed, becomes invisible, or, in Luhmannian terms, is de-paradoxified. An observer observing an observer is not, however, able to simultaneously observe himself as observer and therefore has his own blind spot. This displaces the paradox of observation, but at the same time the nature of the paradox changes to 'a paradox of re-entry'. The paradox on the level of the second order is the fact that the distinction system/environment is, at the same time the same and not the same once the sub-system has separated itself (by copying the distinction system/environment and re-entering it into the system) in order to observe the system as observer (Luhmann, 1993b, pp 763-82). The re-entry implies that a part of the system obtains a higher reflexive capacity than the rest of it.

Perspective

Even though an observer of the second order is simultaneously an observer of the first order, the outlook is nevertheless different:

- On the level of the first order, the outlook is *mono-contextual*. The observer sees what he sees. He makes use of a distinction without being able to distinguish.
- On the level of the second order, the outlook is *poly-contextual*. Although the observer still observes within the framework of a distinction, the observer of observers knows that she cannot see that which she cannot see. She knows that reality depends on the observer – that the observed is contingent with the difference that defines the boundaries of the observation. She uses a distinction but she is also able to distinguish.

- The observer of observers as observers is able to see that his observations of observations do not lead to random results and that the choice of a particular distinction has implications.

In other words, the theory of observation holds *autological* implications. The theory's statements about observation are true of the theory itself. In the words of Elena Esposito:

> [Luhmann's] approach is not simple self-referential but auto-logic, where with ontology one indicates the condition by which the knowing systems is itself one of the objects it has to know: when it describes its object it then also describes itself, and the description modifies the object to be described. (Esposito, 1996)

Luhmann speaks of a radical constructivism that includes itself (Luhmann, 1986, pp 129-34, 1990c).

Conducting systems-theoretical analysis

This requires of the systems-theoretical observer to meticulously substantiate and account for the way she constructs and thus observes her reality of observations (Luhmann, 1988a). As a minimum, a systems theorist must do the following.

Account for and substantiate his choice of guiding distinction

Guiding distinction is understood as that distinction which is defined as the framework for observation of observations. It has great implications for viewing observing observers through the distinction system/environment. The moment one defines the distinction system/environment as the basis of second-order observation, reality is always constructed as *either* system *or* environment. We will then be viewing a system's observations as either referring to the system itself or to the environment of the system. We are encouraged to always see how the observing system divides the world into the system itself and its environment when it observes, that is, how the observing system comes into being through its distinction between system and environment. It is not presupposed that a second-order observer observes with the distinction system/environment. In principle, any difference with the possibility of re-entry into itself can exist as the framework for observations of the second order, and any of these differences hold implications for the construction of reality.

Account for the conditioning of the chosen guiding distinction

In this context, *conditioning* means the definition of conditions of indication. If, for example, we take as our starting point the guiding distinction system/ environment, conditioning means the designation of the conditions of when that which we observe is accepted as a system or the environment of a system respectively. One condition could be that the system itself is able to distinguish between itself and its environment. To reiterate, the systems of the world do no let us know how they wish to be observed; only we can be held accountable for our observations through the explication of the conditions of observation.

Point out, substantiate and account for the implications of the exact observation point

Operating as an observer of the second order with distinctions that can re-enter themselves, it is not self-evident what is defined as object. Even when observing observers through, for example, the distinction system/environment, it remains for the observer to decide which system is defined as the observation point, since all systems simultaneously constitute the environment of other systems. The moment one system has been selected as the observation point, all other systems can only be seen as environment, and only then to the extent that they are constructed as such by the particular system. In the words of Luhmann, any theory about observed systems must designate its *systems reference*:

> which it uses as its starting point in order to designate which system which things exist as the environment of. [...] However, if one wants to know the systems reference upon which an observer is based [...] one must observe the observer. The world does not disclose the way it wants it. With the choice of systems reference, one has simultaneously designated the system which draws its own boundaries and thus divides the world into system and environment. (Luhmann, 1995b, p 46)

For example...

We might be interested in observing observations on national financial management. If we define the Agency of the Environment as our observation point, we will be able to observe, for one thing, the way financial management emerges as an organisational programme for economic decisions within the Agency of the Environment. We will also be able to see how the Agency of the Environment constructs itself as 'environment' in relation to the state, in a distinction between economic factors under its control and economic factors defined by the environment. However, by defining the political system as the observation point, another distinction becomes central – namely politics/administration – and financial management becomes a political battlefield for the control of an administration (including the Agency of the Environment) that is viewed as increasingly ungovernable. Hence, the observation point constitutes what we see and which questions emerge.

This demands self-restriction and precision of gaze, which is implied in Luhmann's systems theory, because of theory about observation as the unity of indication and distinction nevertheless allows for a particular analytical flexibility.

The observer of the second order can always ask:

- Why this particular guiding distinction?
- Why not a different distinction, which could lead to the replacement of the chosen guiding distinction by a different distinction capable of re-entry?

In systems theory there is no concept of essence forcing a second-order observer to view reality in a particular way. Reality, as such, is not observable anyway and does not therefore demand anything specific from the observer. Reality is observer-dependent and in that respect it is a construction and also a reality.

The observer of the second order can also always inquire about the conditioning of the guiding distinction:

- Is it possible to condition the particular guiding distinction differently and more productively?

For example, in his earlier writings Luhmann conditioned social systems as systems of action, but later found it more productive to condition social systems as systems of communication.

Finally, there is always the option of moving the observation point. It is always possible to move backwards in the process of re-entry so that that which was seen as system now appears as sub-system, or move forward in the process of re-entry so that that which was seen as system now appears as environment. This applies, not only to the distinction system/environment, but to all concepts capable of re-entry (that is, all second-order concepts).

I have tried to summarise these notions of observation and observation of the second order in Table 4.1:

Table 4.1: First- versus second-order observation

	Observation of the first order	Observation of the second order
Observation	Observations of something in the world through indication within the framework of a distinction	Observation of observations as observations, that is, observations of the boundaries of indication in other observations within the framework of the same distinction
Reference	External reference	Self-reference
Distinction	Object: this/something else Concepts: concept/counter-concept	Second-order concepts: concept that can appear as part of their own whole, that is, concepts capable of re-entry
Outlook	Mono-contextual	Poly-contextual

Conclusion

Having used a considerable amount of space on Luhmann's concept of observation, I will continue with the rest of this chapter. First, some of the central conditionings of the system/environment distinction that follow the concepts of meaning, consciousness and communication are discussed. Then, some of the alternative guiding distinctions in Luhmann's systems theory are introduced, which exist in addition to the system/environment distinction.

The concept of meaning

Luhmann's theory of observation avoids any kind of anthropocentrism. Not only people observe: the observing system could be anything from a thermostat in a refrigerator, or an organic cell to a national bureaucracy. With the theory of observation, therefore, we have only just begun. Thus, we must move on to specify which type of system we are fundamentally interested in. What is our systems reference? Although an organic cell is as capable of observation as a bureaucracy, their systemic conditions of observation are obviously very different. Luhmann's general systems theory assumes that all systems are autopoietic, meaning that they themselves create the elements they consist of, including the constitutive boundary between system and environment. On this general level, systems can be compared to the basic element of autopoiesis. Luhmann distinguishes between organic systems, psychic systems and social systems – organic systems create themselves through *life*, whereas psychic and social systems create themselves through *meaning*.

Meaning

When focusing on *social* systems, meaning thus becomes the first inevitable concept. In part, the concept of meaning plays the same part in Luhmann's systems theory as the concept of discoursivity plays in Laclau's discourse theory:

- While all social identities in Laclau are embedded in a discoursivity and are unable to go beyond this discoursivity, psychic and social systems in Luhmann are similarly unable to operate outside of meaning.
- In the same way that discoursivity in Laclau is constituted by differences and relations, meaning in Luhmann is also a concept of difference.
- Finally, while discoursivity in Laclau is characterised by floating and unfixable relationships between discursive elements, meaning in Luhmann is similarly unfixable, and is always unstable and indefinable.

However, having defined these similarities, the differences become clear. In fact, the lines of reasoning behind the indicated similarities are very different.

Although both theorists relate meaning to difference, this conclusion is based on different approaches. In Laclau, meaning is not founded on an external referential relationship, either in capacity of an external reality or as sign structure. Meaning is neither a structuralist nor a poststructuralist concept. The main inspiration behind Luhmann's concept of meaning stems from Husserl's phenomenology: "The best way to approach the meaning of meaning might well be the phenomenological method. This is by no means equivalent to taking a subjective or even psychological stance. On the contrary, phenomenology means: taking the world as it appears without asking ontological or metaphysical questions" (Luhmann, 1985, p 101).

Luhmann defines meaning simply as the unity of the distinction *actuality/ potentiality* (Luhmann, 1995c, p 65). At the particular moment that something appears central to the thought or to the communication, something is actualised, but this always happens in relation to a horizon of possible actualisations (that is, potentiality). There is always a predefined core surrounded by references to other possibilities that cannot be used simultaneously. It is important not to understand potentiality or possibility as structures that precede actualisation, but as a horizon that lines up with actualisation – something appears and thereby excludes other possibilities. Thus, meaning is the simultaneous presentation of actuality and potentiality. Meaning is the actual surrounded by possibilities; any actualisation of the moment potentialises new possibilities.

For example...

I decide to write a chapter on Luhmann and, simultaneously, a horizon arises of alternative constructivists who could have been the object of my interest: Bourdieu, Latour, Castoriades and so on. I choose to begin with the theory of observation and immediately a horizon of other points of departures emerges: for example, the concept of autopoeisis or the concept of society. As soon as something is actualised, meaning can be extended by connecting, in a new selection of meaning, to the actualised side or by crossing across the difference and actualising something that was formerly potential. For example, I can decide that it was the wrong decision to begin with the concept of observation and that the concept of society would be the better choice. Consequently, the actual and the potential cannot be separated but can only exist in simultaneous relationships with each other. In Luhmann's words: "Meaning is the link between the actual and the possible: it is not one or the other" (Luhmann, 1985, p 102).

Meaning and psychic and social systems

Psychic and social systems are tied to meaning. They possess no relationship with the environment, let alone themselves, except through meaning. Meaning is the shape of the world and overrules the distinction between system and environment. On the other hand, there are no limits to meaning as such – in principle, anything can be understood by psychic and social systems but only within the shape of meaning. Meaning can never extend itself into something else (Luhmann, 1995c, pp 59-63). Hence, meaning is open-ended in the sense that everything can be understood through meaning, but it is closed and self-referential in the sense that meaning refers only to meaning.

Like discursive identity in Laclau, meaning can never be fixed. However, Luhmann's argument for this is not that a structure is not complete but that the core of the actualised disintegrates from the moment something has been indicated. Meaning can never be fixed or maintained; it is fundamentally unstable. This is in part due to the fact that meaning is always shaped by a thought or by communication, which disappears the very moment it occurs. Meaning is always reproduced (or changed) recursively, like decisions within an organisation.

For example...

It is always decided at the following meeting, when the minutes are being approved, which decisions are not to be considered decisions after all but simply talk, and which decisions are to be included in the minutes and should therefore be followed up and put on the agenda in terms of new decisions. However, the decisions included in the minutes can never be identical to the decisions as they emerged at the previous meeting. They now appear in a new situation, in a new specification in relation to a new horizon of possibilities: for example, the possibility of the minutes not being approved, or of the decisions not really being decided upon. The core of actuality thus disintegrates from the moment it appears and, consequently, meaning provokes change.

Meaning, therefore, is also a continuing rearranging of the difference between actuality and possibility (Luhmann, 1995c, pp 63-6).

This implies, moreover, that social and psychic systems are dynamic systems that never stay identical to themselves; they always exist in a movement of becoming. In Luhmann's words, the actual is secure but unstable. The potential, in turn, is stable but insecure. The option of stable security does not exist (Luhmann, 1985, p 102).

The concept of communication

Meaning is constituted by psychic as well as social systems, and is a collective medium for the two systems. Psychic systems operate in terms of meaning in the shape of a closed connection of consciousness. Social systems operate in terms of meaning in the shape of a closed connection of communication.

The distinction between psychic and social systems is crucial to Luhmann's theory of society as communication. Any common-sense perspective would maintain that communication must necessarily be between people, but also that only people are able to communicate. Contrary to this view, Luhmann argues:

- First, within a systems perspective, people cannot even be indicated as a unit, they are, in the words of Kneer and Nassehi, "a plurality of independent systems – eg, the organic system, the immune system, the neurophysiological system, and the psychic system all of which operate without any overlap between them whatsoever" (Kneer and Nassehi, 1993, p 70).
- Second, Luhmann argues that, fundamentally speaking, people cannot communicate at all, not even in their capacity of psychic systems. Communication alone is able to communicate (Luhmann, 1996, p 261).

Autopoietic systems

The background for this view is Luhmann's understanding of systems as *autopoietic systems*. The fact that a system is autopoietic means that it invents itself and everything that it consists of:

> Everything that is used as a unit by the system is produced by the system itself. This applies to elements, processes, boundaries, and other structures and, last but not least, to the unity of the system itself. Autopoietic systems, then, are sovereign with respect to the constitution of identities and differences. They, of course, do not create a material world of their own. They presuppose other levels of reality, as for example human life presupposes the small span of temperature in which water is liquid. But whatever they use as identity and differences is of their own making. (Luhmann, 1990b, p 3)

The strength of the concept of autopoiesis lies in the possibility of an unambiguous perspective on society and its social systems as an independent thing that cannot be reduced to something other than itself, for example to consciousness or a sum of actions. Again, we see the phenomenological insistence on observing society as it appears without reference to conditions external to society.

Psychic systems belong to the environment of social systems. They are autopoietic systems that produce meaning in a closed connection of consciousness by the process of thoughts connecting with other thoughts. A psychic system can never extend itself beyond itself. It is unable to connect with the thoughts of a different psychic system. Hence, psychic systems are unable to ever obtain a mutual understanding, let alone a fusion of their meaning horizons, partial or complete. In this sense, it is not possible for psychic systems to communicate with each other.

Conversely, social systems also belong to the environment of psychic systems. Social systems are autopoietic and produce meaning in a closed connection of communication by connecting communication with other communication. Likewise, social systems are unable to extend themselves beyond themselves. Communication cannot connect with thoughts but only with communication. No consciousness, therefore, can be completely identical to communication, and no communication can be completely identical to consciousness.

Nevertheless, social and psychic systems are structurally linked: first, they both shape meaning as a medium (but in different forms); second, they make their own complexity available to each other. Although psychic systems are unable to communicate with each other, communication is also unable to communicate unless at least two psychic systems partake in the communication. Social systems, in turn, make their complexity available to psychic systems, primarily through language and through disappointment/fulfilment of the expectations of psychic systems.

Information, form and understanding

To Luhmann, communication is understood not as acts of communication (since he would then be reducing social systems to human acts) nor as the transfer of messages between sender and receiver (not even in the more reception-oriented version). Rather, the notion of communication in Luhmann is to be seen as a kind of coordinated selection. Communication is a selection process, consisting of a synthesis of three selections:

1. Selection of *information*, that is, what is to be communicated.
2. Selection of *form of message*, that is, how the information is to be communicated.
3. Selection of *understanding*, that is, what should be understood about the message (Luhmann, 1995c, pp 137-176).

Communication does not become communication until all three selection processes have occurred. Monologues, for example, are not communication – the message needs to be understood before it can be regarded as communication. In this context, it is important to stress that the concept of understanding does not refer to the reception of the message by a psychic system but instead to the linking up to the message by subsequent communication.

Communication

Any message establishes a horizon of possible links to new communication. Subsequent communication links up to the message by actualising one of these possibilities and by leaving the others as a horizon of potentiality. Thus, understanding is nothing other than the retrospective choice of connection by subsequent communication.

Therefore, it requires at least two communications in order for communication to exist.

It should be noted that the three selections noted above all shape meaning as a medium. The selection of information shapes the distinction of actualised information/possible information; the selection of message shapes the distinction of actualised message/possible messages; and the selection of understanding shapes the distinction of actualised connection/possible connections.

Also, it should be noted that communication is self-referential. Communication connects with previous communication and, in this sense, social systems arise in the recursivity of communication.

Preliminary summary

As we have seen, Luhmann's systems theory is a theory about society as communication. It assumes that society consists of autopoietic systems of communication, which produce and reproduce themselves through communication alone. The different systems of communication are closed around themselves; they are self-referring. And this closure constitutes the condition of their openness, that is, of their sensitivity to their environment.

All communication is observation, either in the shape of self-description or external descriptions. The closure of systems of communication both in regard to meaning and to communication implies that systems of communication always observe from a blind spot.

Systems theory attempts to establish itself as observation of the second order – as an observation of how systems of communication observe. It is about the description of the limits and blind spots (in the broadest sense) of communication. It is not only a question of describing how a system of communication sees something and not something else. It is also not only a question of localising the moment when silence takes over. But it is concerned with the relationship between the different systems of communication, the way they are connected, the way they interrupt each other productively and destructively, including the existing limits, not only of the individual system of communication, but also of the overall communication structure of society.

As a second-order observer, systems theory must recognise that it is itself communication within society. In that sense, systems theory is about contributing to the self-description of society but, as part of society, systems theory is faced with a classical sociological problem: self-reference. Within systems theory, autology provides the solution to this problem of self-reference. Through the concept of autology, systems theory can describe itself as a form of self-description describing itself. An autological sociological description of society in society thus describes the description of society by adapting it to itself. This means, for one thing, that systems theory explores its own origins, but it also means that it has to define explicitly those guiding differences on which it bases its second-order observations, and account for the way they construct the object of systems theory.

The next section presents some of the central guiding distinctions to observation of the second order in Luhmann's systems theory.

Form analysis

When taking the concept of observation as the point of departure, it is important to grant priority to Luhmann's form analysis. It appears that all choices and accounts of choices in Luhmann begin with a form analysis of the guiding distinction itself. The role of form analysis in relation to systems analysis in a broader sense is highly comparable to the role of deconstruction in the analysis of hegemony in Laclau.

While deconstruction in Laclau focuses on specific central dualities around which a discursive game is played out, form analysis similarly focuses on specific distinctions in connection to which communication plays itself out. The deconstruction of central dualities produces particular logicities, which necessarily emerge in certain discourses. Likewise, form analysis analyses the boundaries of communication and the paradoxes that communication unfolds when it connects with one particular distinction.

Luhmann defines form as the *unity* of a difference. This brings us back to the theory of observation but now we have specified the systems reference to social, meaning-shaping systems of communication.

For example...

We observe the observations of an observer and note that the observer focuses on, for example, the risks of nuclear power. We might also note that other observers focus on different risks – the risk of prenatal diagnosis, of share investments, of work and so on. We notice a certain recursivity in the communication, when questions of risk appear. We now need to ask whether a particular *form* of communication appears to define itself within societal communication, which we can call 'risk communication'.

- If this communication is characterised by its ability to indicate risks, then what are the conditions of its existence?

If we pose this question in terms of form analysis, the objective is at first to localise the difference, which defines the scope of the indication of risks.

- Which difference allows an observer to see the environment in terms of risks?

The question becomes more specific:

- Which is the unmarked side of the difference when communication indicates risk?

Consequently, form analysis is the analysis of the conditions of communication given a specific difference, the guiding distinction of form analysis being unity/difference.

Luhmann himself uses the example of risk (Luhmann, 1990d) and asks if the other side of the difference might be security. Security/risk is a distinction that is often related to risk communication; however, Luhmann rejects this proposal, since security cannot be conditioned and cannot therefore operate as counter-concept to risk. In other words, it is not able to describe the blind spot of risk communication. Instead, Luhmann suggests 'danger' is the other side of risk. Risk communication is subsequently defined as communication that connects with the distinction risk/danger. If communication connecting with risk shapes the distinction risk/danger, then risk is always only risk in relation to a danger. Risk and danger cannot be separated but only exist in relation to each other. Now the distinction has been identified. The subsequent form analysis asks which kind of communication can develop within the scope of this distinction.

- What must necessarily follow the shaping of this very distinction?
- What are the restrictions on communication due to this distinction?

It is precisely the question of the *unity* of the distinction. Luhmann's answer to this question in relation to risk communication is too far-reaching to be included here, but he demonstrates, among other things, how communication, which produces decisions by ascribing risk to the decision itself, simultaneously assigns an unspecified danger to others.

For example...

One driver's decision to assign himself the risk of passing another car on a curve at high speed on the assumption that he can just make it simultaneously implies the assignment of danger to others. Danger exists in being exposed to the risk decisions of others (Luhmann, 1990d).

In accordance with Derrida and deconstruction, one might say that form analysis points to a particular 'logicity' given a specific guiding difference in the communication. Where deconstruction tries to convert the hierarchy of differences, form analysis begins by inquiring about the other side of the side indicated. Form analysis tries to locate the distinction that constitutes the framework of a particular observation. Subsequently, form analysis inquires about the unity of the distinction and hence about the communication that the distinction both enables and excludes. Luhmann has conducted a great number of form analyses, for example on the form of writing, the form of the distinction system/environment, the form of knowledge and the form of causality.

It is important to note that form analysis rarely represents the end of the involvement with a particular problem but often represents the beginning of the formulation of a problem, which is then followed up in other analytics, for example in a systems and differentiation analysis. Luhmann himself defines the difference between form analysis and deconstruction by saying that, where deconstruction often contents itself with uncovering the logicity and paradoxical basis of a duality, form analysis simply constitutes the incipient inquiry about the unfolding of a paradox within communication. Given the fact that, for example, the concept of risk is paradoxical by nature (since communication on risk is itself risky, whoever runs a risk and inflicts danger on others runs the risk of becoming visible), how and within which systems of communication is this paradox handled? In this respect, we can trace a certain parallel to Laclau to whom deconstruction is merely the beginning of an analysis of hegemony.

Systems analysis

The most central guiding distinction in Luhmann is the distinction *system/ environment*. It is not only the difference most often used by Luhmann in his second-order observations, it is also the difference he uses to regulate the use of other guiding distinctions and, more generally, to steer his development of theories.

In systems analysis, the basic notion is that all communication takes place within a social system, and that all social systems are constituted by a boundary of system and environment. As indicated in relation to the theory of observation, it is the very observation that divides the world into system and environment. The same pertains to social systems in which observations consist in communicative descriptions. A social system can observe itself or the environment through descriptions of self-reference or external reference. One example of self-referential communication in an organisation is financial accounting in the same way that surveys of waste sites are examples of communication of external reference in environmental administrations.

The very construction of the distinction system/environment as a guiding distinction for second-order observation begins with a form analysis of the distinction, that is, with an analysis of the capacity of communication to shape the distinction system/environment. For one thing, form analysis demonstrates that the environment always works as an environment of a particular system and, conversely, that a system is always a system only in relation to a specific environment. *A social system is simply the unity of the distinction system/environment.* When communication recursively connects with communication, social systems emerge because of the distinction by the communication between self-reference and external reference – between that which constitutes the system itself and that which makes up the environment of the system.

Both system and environment are internal structures of communication. Environment is not 'reality' as such: environment consists of that which is defined by the communication as its relevant surroundings. The system, in turn, is only a system in relation to this internal construction of the environment. System is that which environment is not. Any system therefore is identical with itself in its difference (and only in the difference) from the internal environment construction.

A second-order observation, employing as its guiding difference the distinction system/environment, is thus an observation of *the way in which a social system creates itself in the construction of its environment through communicative descriptions*. It is an observation of how a system distinguishes between system and environment when it observes.

The difference between system and environment is the *boundary of meaning* of the social system. The boundary system/environment is not spatial or material: it pertains to the space of possibility for the creation of meaning in the system. Any social system constitutes an autopoietic system of meaning of its own, which produces meaning according to individual rules of selection. The boundary of meaning indicates that there are different conditions of the creation of meaning inside and outside the system. An observation of a system's use in its observations of a certain distinction between system and environment is thus simultaneously a second-order observation of the limits to the creation of meaning within a specific system, that is, the way in which a system ascribes meaning to itself and its environment.

In this way, each social system is autopoietic both in respect to communication and meaning. Accordingly, communication can only take place within a social system and never between social systems. Social systems are unable to communicate *with* each other but are able to communicate about each other.

Differentiation analysis

As we have already seen, the distinction system/environment is not merely a difference, but one that has the capacity for re-entry into itself. A social system comes into being through a communicative installation of a boundary between system and environment. However, this is a formation *within* society as a social system of communication. Any formation of a social system consists, therefore, of a transcription of the difference system/environment and its re-entry into the system itself. Hence, social systems come into being as differentiations of communication (see Figure 4.6).

Figure 4.6: Re-entry of the distinction system/environment

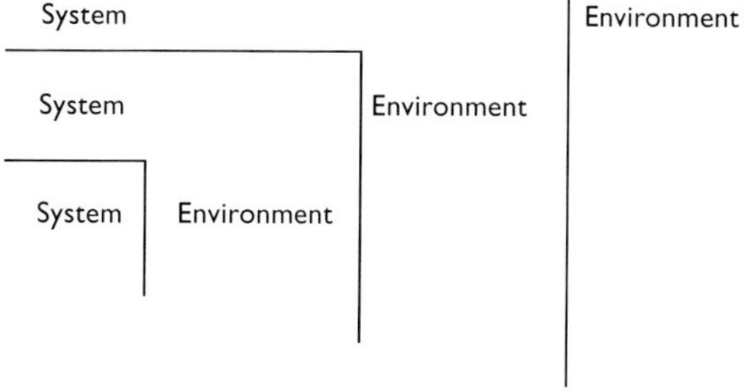

The differentiation of social systems implies the creation of distinct communication forms of different perspectives of observation. The social systems observe their difference from within their scope and each in its own way splits the world in two through the distinction system/environment. Thus, the world becomes poly-contextual.

Although any social system exists as a sub-system in society, it is not a part of a whole. Society can never be represented as a whole; there is no total sum of the perspectives of observation of the different social systems. On the contrary, society becomes environment to the sub-systems and does so differently in relation to each of the sub-systems. Any differentiation defines the system from which it is differentiated as its environment.

Another reason for the impossibility of describing society as a unified whole is the fact that a description of society is based on one specific system and has one systems-relative way of creating meaning. Luhmann's assertion is that we are able to observe the similarities in the way in which the social systems' perspectives of observation are differentiated. This is termed the *form of differentiation*, that is, the unity of the difference between the systems.

Above the guiding distinction system/environment, we see, therefore, the guiding difference *similarity/difference*. The second-order observation in the differentiation analysis is the observation of the similarity of the difference between system and environment in social systems. The question is how are systems differentiated by virtue of the re-entry into themselves of the system/ environment distinction? That is, in which way do the social systems become parts of their own whole? This pertains to the similarity in the mutual dissimilarity of the systems' construction of themselves and their environment. The analysis of the form of differentiation does not merely suggest the constitution of the possibilities for communication in one particular system, but also the general possibilities and limitations for the formation of perspectives of observation and for social systems of communication given a specific form of differentiation.

Luhmann traces a shift in the overall form of differentiation in society in the direction of functional differentiation, which reveals new forms of communication while simultaneously excluding other previous forms. Within the segmented form of differentiation, society is differentiated into identical sub-systems – there are numerous social systems but they all constitute themselves in the same way with the same perspective of observation. Within the stratified form of differentiation, the social systems are segregated by layers, such as, for example, the caste system of old Indian societies, or citizens versus slaves in Ancient Greece, or the kings, nobility, peasantry and tenants of European feudal society. Within the functional form of differentiation, social systems are differentiated in respect of their functions, for example the financial system, which is centred on the function of price fixing, or the political system, which is centred on collective decisions, or the educational system, which is centred on separation. This does not indicate whether or not the functionally differentiated society is actually functional. Indeed, there is considerable evidence to the contrary.

For example, Luhmann points out that the closure brought about by the communicative focus on functions blinds society to the destruction of the ecological precondition of society by the function systems. Each individual form of differentiation only allows for particular perspectives of observation, which is the same as saying that each form of differentiation installs its blind spot within the communication of society. One example of a perspective of observation that can exist in the stratified society but not in functional society is the male-dominated perspective of observation. Formerly, the distinction between man and woman made up a guiding difference in respect of social stratification. Within the functionally differentiated society, the asymmetric indication of the male side and the use of the distinction man/woman as a principle of differentiation for social systems are no longer useful in the same way.

Table 4.2: The differentiation of society

Segmental differentiation	Similar sub-systems, such as tribes, villages and families	
Stratified differentiation	Differentiation in uneven layers based on the difference top/bottom	
Functional differentiation	Differentiation in dissimilar sub-systems that differ from each other in respect to their function in society	

Points of observation

Although Luhmann has primarily studied the form of differentiation of *society*, there is no reason why one should not choose other *points of observation*. The point of observation could be a specific organisational system for an examination of how sub-systems are differentiated; it could be the public administration to consider changes in differentiation form from a formal administration to an administration divided into different sectors and, hence, changes in the autopoiesis of the administration; or it could be changes in the differentiation form of news media from party press via regional press to broadsheets versus tabloid newpapers. In other words, the object of the differentiation analysis depends entirely on the choice of systems reference.

Media analysis

A fourth analytics of Luhmann draws on the guiding difference *form/medium*. Any observation is an observation by a system in which observation exists in an indication within the scope of a distinction. Subsequently, any observation forms differences or, rather, any observation establishes a relationship between observation as form and its difference as medium. In order for an observation to be brought about in the first place, difference as difference has to offer itself up as medium for a form that can condense differences into specific forms such as horse/not horse, right/wrong, car/not car. Differences as loose elements, without preferences one way or the other and open to any consolidation, make up the medium of observation, which can precisely only take place by isolating a single form in the medium of difference. If we look at Spencer-Brown's form calculus reproduced in Figure 4.7, we can see that the very line or gibbet is the medium of form as the unity of the specific separation of m from not m.

Figure 4.7: The calculus of form

By *media*, Luhmann understands loosely coupled elements. Media are characterised by a high resolution and by being accessible to Gestalt fixations (Luhmann, 1986b, p 101). Conversely, *form* to Luhmann implies a fixed connection of elements: "Forms emerge [...] through a condensation of the mutual dependency between elements, that is, through the selection of the possibilities offered up by a medium" (Luhmann, 1986b, p 102). Moreover, media always consist of numerous elements:

> Forms, on the contrary, reduce size to that which they can order. No medium creates only one form since it would then be absorbed and disappear. The combinatory possibilities of a medium can never be exhausted and the only reason for restrictions to evolve is the fact that the creations of forms mutually disrupt each other. (Luhmann, 1986b, p 101)

The relationship between form and medium is itself a form, meaning that any speech on form is only form in relation to a medium and vice versa. Forms are only shaped when a medium makes itself available but, on the other hand, form prevails in relation to the medium, without any resistance on the part of the medium in regard to the rigidity of form. The difference between form and medium, however, is relative in the sense that form can be more or less rigid.

For example...

One example of a medium is money, which is a medium precisely because payments can:

> be offered as random notes, because one payment does not depend on the significance and purpose of another payment, because the medium is incredibly forgetful (since it does not have to remember in order to maintain the paid amount), and because the solvency determines whether payment is possible. (Luhmann, 1986b, p 101)

Decisions are an example of form; they constitute a form because they impress themselves in a medium and condense its elements into one decision, which is only a decision in relation to previous decisions and decisions not taken. The decision to print the company's logo on paper forms the medium of money by requiring expenditure. This decision is not interchangeable with other decisions – its meaning is tied to time and space, and can only be understood in relation to the company's other decisions. Moreover, the decision has been made possible by previous decisions, for example the decision to have a company logo.

A form is not necessarily tied to one medium. It is possible to imagine a situation in which several media make themselves available to the same form. An organisation can form numerous different media (for example, money, law and power), although it can never do so simultaneously.

Which forms and media are available to communication is an historical question, that is to say, the difference between form and medium varies historically. Furthermore, the distinction form/medium is capable of re-entry so that a specific form can later work as medium for a new form. This extends to an evolutionary question about the way media arise and produce possibilities for new forms of communication. In the words of Luhmann:

> How language, how writing, how alphabetical writing, and how symbolically generalised media appear. They provide a potential for the creation of forms which would not exist without them, and we can take advantage of this potential as soon as the social conditions permit it. (Luhmann, 1986b, p 104)

Historically, we can trace a development in which forms have, over time, become media of new forms. In theory, the only limit is the fact that media cannot be developed beyond the communication of form. Thus, the number and ways of forms and media offering themselves to communication is fundamentally an empirical question. As a result of the historical evolution of new media, one could possibly speak of a media/form staircase on which the next step is open (see Figure 4.8). Distinction is the medium for the form of meaning, which further constitutes the medium for the form of language, which in turn works as the medium for media of distribution and so on. The staircase is by no means complete.

The implications of this extend to how we observe observations whose guiding distinction is form/medium. The capacity of distinctions for re-entry entails numerous potential points of observation. As with the guiding distinction system/environment, the point of observation can always be moved forwards or backwards. With the guiding distinction system/environment, one is always able to choose a new systems reference, and with the guiding distinction form/medium one can always choose a new form reference. Depending on what we define as form in our second-order observation, different relationships appear as medium (although no medium will appear, of course, if there are no

Figure 4.8: Media/form staircase

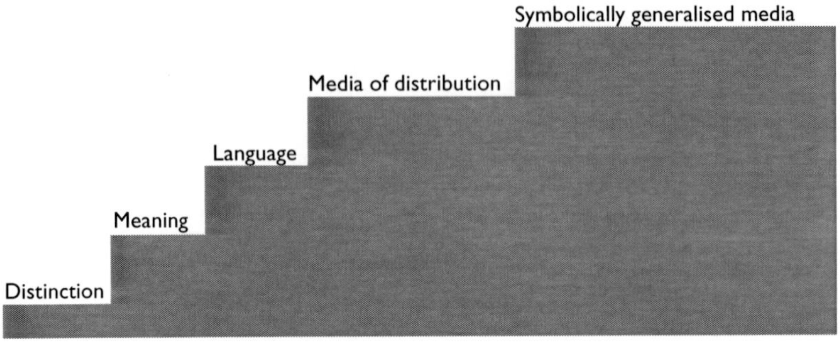

media). Luhmann provides the following example: "A public organisation can be considered a form but also a medium in which interests clash and impress themselves" (Luhmann, 1986b, p 104).

As we have already suggested above, Luhmann's theory of society ascribes a more prominent position to some media than to others. As a principle rule, he distinguishes between three types of communication media:

- language;
- media of distribution, such as writing and television;
- general symbolic media, such as, for example, money.

He only ascribes binary codes to the general communication media.

Semantic analysis

Finally, Luhmann employs semantic analysis, which forms the guiding distinction *condensation/meaning*, to examine how meaning is condensed in semantic forms that produce a conceptual pool for communication.

Luhmann makes a distinction between system and semantics in which semantics are defined as particular structures linking communication to communication by offering up forms of meaning that systems of communication treat as worth preserving (Luhmann, 1995c, p 282).

If we were to invoke the concept of discourse anywhere in Luhmann's theoretical architecture, this would be the place. In the same way that we can talk about different discourses in Foucault that enable the enunciation of particular discursive objects, Luhmann speaks of different semantics (the semantics of love, of organisational theory, of money and so on) that invoke specific communication. However, the distinction between system and semantics is considerably different to Foucault's concept of discourse. In Foucault, a discourse can contain characteristics of system; a discourse can constitute a regime and a discourse can conflict with other discourses; discourses possess qualities of reality. Semantics do not in the same way posseses these qualities. They do not have a self; they cannot make up a regime; they cannot conflict with each other. Only systems hold the characteristics of system; systems decide whether or not they wish to employ specific semantics. Consequently, semantics do not exist by themselves outside the systems of communication. An observer can choose to make a semantic distinction between system and structure but they cannot actually be separated. The semantic structures are used and reproduced in the selection of communication that is linked to communication, and can only exist in the constriction of choices.

The concept of semantics is based on a distinction between *meaning* and *condensed meaning*. As noted above, meaning comprises a constant rearranging of the distinction actuality/potentiality. Meaning disintegrates immediately on its actualisation. Thus, meaning is tied to the momentary condition of actualisation. Communication, on the other hand, is capable of developing structures that condense meaning into forms, which are set free from the momentary condition of actualisation. Condensation means that a multitude of meaning is captured in a single form, which subsequently makes itself available to an undefined communication. Consequently, semantics are characterised as *the accumulated amount of generalised forms of differences (for example, concepts, ideas, images, and symbols) available for the selection of meaning within the systems of communication*. In other words, semantics are condensed and repeatable forms of meaning, which are at our disposal for communication. These generalised forms are relatively independent of situations and obtain their specific content from the communication by which they are selected (Luhmann, 1993c, pp 9-72). This definition of semantics largely derives from Koselleck's history of concepts.

Objects and concepts are among the forms that semantics can take. As noted previously, objects constitute a form that has an undefined outer side (for example, horse/not horse). The concept, in turn, is a form of meaning in which the indicated inner side delineates restrictions for the outer side (for example, man/woman), and hence concepts are inextricably bound up with counter-concepts. There exist no concepts without counter-concepts and thus no unambiguous concepts (Luhmann, 1988b, pp 47-117).

Luhmann distinguishes between three dimensions of meaning (Luhmann, 1995c, pp 74-82), which enables him to distinguish accordingly between three forms of semantics. We will not go into this distinction in depth but merely give a brief précis:

- The *fact dimension* pertains to the selection of themes and objects for communication and consciousness. Themes and objects are all designed according to the distinction this/something else in the same way as 'object' as a form of meaning. Similarly, we can speak of semantics of facts as generalised forms of 'being-one-thing-and-not-another'.
- The *social dimension* is based on non-identity in the relationship between communicators and constitutes the horizon of possibility in the tension between 'alter' and 'ego'. It thus concerns that which cannot be regarded

as oneself. Semantically, it relates to generalised forms of differences between 'us' and 'them'. There can be no 'us' without being in comparison with a 'them'.

- Finally, the *temporal dimension* articulates the tension between past and future. The temporal dimension is "constituted by the fact that the difference between before and after, which can be immediately experienced in all events, is referred to specific horizons, namely extended into past and future" (Luhmann, 1995c, p 78). The semantics of time concern the ways in which we observe and conceptualise past and future. Much like in Koselleck, past, present and future cannot be regarded as given entities. On the contrary, they are construed in and by communication and in every communication. In the words of Luhmann: "What moves in time is past/present/future together, in other words, the present along with its past and future horizons" (Luhmann, 1982, p 307).

Connections between the different analytics

Once we have understood the guiding differences presented above, the emerging question concerns the connections between them. Here, I must admit to finding myself on thin ice. This chapter on Luhmann has introduced a total of five central analytics (as compared to, for example, the chapter on Laclau, which covered only two), and I do not believe that Luhmann has ever fully elaborated on the overall connections between these. There are three reasons for this. First of all, the rudimentary attempts that have been made to describe the connections between the guiding principles are far from having been revised in relation to the Spencer-Brownian turn in Luhmann's writings. Second, the descriptions of connections are not coherent across his different books (possibly for the same reason). Third, it is possible that Luhmann does not fundamentally believe in the possibility of one joint analytical strategy and maintains that the different analytics combine to constitute a flexible structure whose composition depends on the problem.

The following conclusions are based on the third of the above reasons and will consider the numerous guiding principles as a pool, rather than as distinct elements of one analytical strategy. One possibility is to conduct a systematic reading of the connections between the guiding differences in Luhmann's different analyses. That would be an interesting study in itself, but beyond the scope of this book. Instead, I will provide some examples of how the guiding differences are brought together in different analytical strategies.

Form analysis and semantic analysis

The relationship between these analyses has a strong resemblance to the relationship between deconstruction and the analysis of hegemony in Laclau. Form analysis analyses the unity of a concept and illustrates the concept's foundation on a paradoxical distinction. The semantic analysis is then able to employ the paradox as a guiding principle in tracing the history of specific semantics: the semantics of love, the semantics of law and so on. Subsequently, semantic history acts as a history of the de-paradoxification of a particular paradox, for example the history of how the paradox of the justice of justice has historically sought de-paradoxification through different judicial semantics: natural law, judicial positivism, Scandinavian judicial realism and so on. Historical semantic analysis can, in turn, point out new concepts for form analysis. The relationship between form analysis and historical semantic analysis is illustrated in Figure 4.9.

Figure 4.9: The relationship between form analysis and semantic analysis

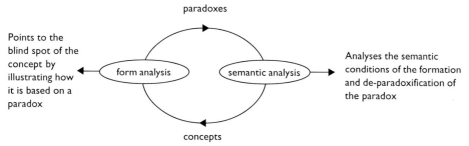

paradoxes

Points to the blind spot of the concept by illustrating how it is based on a paradox

form analysis

semantic analysis

Analyses the semantic conditions of the formation and de-paradoxification of the paradox

concepts

Semantics and differentiation

Luhmann provides an explicit description of this relationship in his first book on social structure and semantics (1993c). He understands social structure to mean the relationship between complexity and the primary differentiation form of society. This is based on the notion that the differentiation form of society determines the level of complexity in society (I have chosen to leave out the concept of complexity in my reading of Luhmann). Translated into those concepts that I have chosen to actualise here, the concept means that the differentiation form of society determines the character of the meaning boundary of the social systems, and thus their openness and sensitivity to their environment. In other words, the form of differentiation governs how social systems can be disturbed by their internally constructed environments, and how they react to these disturbances. Accordingly, Luhmann's hypothesis is that semantic development always follows the differentiation form of society, that is, that compression of meaning into concepts in individual social systems follow each other in parallel movements. Luhmann calls this a collective transformation of the semantic apparatuses of society. Accordingly, semantic analysis meets the complexity–differentiation relationship horizontally (see Figure 4.10).

This structure invokes an analytical strategy that explores various semantics related to different social systems (for example, law, politics, art and religion), according to the thesis that simultaneous transformational ruptures in the history of semantics indicate a transformation of the social structure. The

Figure 4.10: The relationship between differentiation and semantics

Complexity

Semantics

Differentiation

Source: Luhmann, 1993c, p 34

relationship between differentiation analysis and semantic analysis is thus defined as a relationship between synchronic and diachronic analysis.

This, in turn, does not mean that Luhmann assumes a figure of continuity in regard to the development of semantics or the existence of a one-to-one relationship between differentiation form and semantics. Semantics change continuously as well as discontinuously in relation to the differentiation form, in the same way that semantics can follow a temporal rhythm different to that of the differentiation form. Concepts and ideas from one form of differentiation can live on in the next one. Concepts can change with the development of new counter-concepts but maintain their designation. Finally, former distinctions can be put together and condensed in the same concept (Luhmann, 1993c, pp 7-8). However, Luhmann maintains the thesis that the form of differentiation fundamentally defines the conditions of development for semantics and not the reverse. The reasons for this appear logical: semantics are shaped and transformed by communication, which is always communication within a social system, and the form of differentiation, as it is, is nothing more than the similarity of the dissimilarity of the social systems[1].

Systems analysis and media analysis

In my opinion, the relationship between systems analysis and media analysis can be presented in different ways. Here, the relationship between the two analyses is defined as an analytical strategy, whose purpose it is to capture the formation of a social system.

The basic notion is that systems of communication always emerge in relation to a medium. Systems of communication are always shaped within a particular medium; there are no social systems except through the formation of a medium, at least the medium of meaning. Luhmann's thesis is that the historical evolution of new media makes the formation of new social systems possible. The study of how a new social system arises, therefore, should always begin with an analysis of the media-related conditions of the emergence of that system. Thus, the evolution of media of diffusion (such as printed media, radio and television) can be viewed as an evolutionary justification of the origin of the mass media system. Correspondingly, the formation of the economic function system presupposes the evolution of money as a general symbolic medium of communication.

Within this analytical strategy, media analysis thus constitutes a study of the historical evolution of media and their justification of new forms of communication. In relation to this, systems analysis becomes a study of how a particular system comes into being through the connection to new evolutionary potentials of the media, and how it establishes its own autopoiesis. This analytical strategy is illustrated in Figure 4.11.

Figure 4.11: The relationship between systems analysis and media analysis

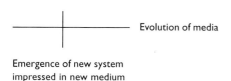

Luhmann's guiding distinctions could create several other analytical strategies, but the three introduced above can serve as an indication of others that are possible.

Conclusion

This chapter has examined the most central analytical strategies in Luhmann's systems theory. I have attempted to summarise these strategies in Table 4.3, and have supplemented them with a specific example. The left-hand column indicates the analytical strategy; the centre column the general inquiry of the analytical strategies; and the right-hand column an example of a potential systems theoretical analysis. The example used in this table concerns the politicisation of businesses. Today, private businesses have become central political players in a number of fields and are expected to take on social responsibility that exceeds purely economic concerns. Today, corporations are expected to consider issues beyond those that are economic; for example, many businesses have developed extensively into areas including ethics, the environment and human rights. Many businesses also take an active role in political decision-making processes; for example, thousands of businesses take part in standardisation committees and commissions, and are involved in decision making about the rules for the European market. These decisions concern consumer interests, the environment, working conditions, industrial policies and much more.

Table 4.3: Luhmann's analytical strategies

Analytical strategy	General question	Example
Form analysis	What is the unity of the distinction? And which paradox does it establish?	In what way are organisations systems that communicate through the form 'decision'? And which paradoxes does this form establish?
Systems analysis	How does a system of communication come into being in a distinction between system and environment? How is the system's boundary of meaning and autopoiesis defined?	In what way does the politicisation of the organisations become apparent in the internal construction by the organisations of their environment so that they not only construct the environment as market but also as political public?
Differentiation analysis	How are systems differentiated? What is the similarity in the dissimilarities of the systems? What are the conditions, therefore, of the formation of new systems of communication?	In what way does the politicisation of the organisations challenge their internal form of differentiation and force them to institutionalise internal reflections of themselves as closed communication (for example, through the establishment of so-called 'ethics officers')?
Semantic analysis	How is meaning condensed? And how does it create a pool of forms, that is, stable and partially general distinctions available to the systems of communication?	How is meaning condensed with respect to environment, human rights, ethics, animal welfare, health and prevention, into the concept of 'the socially responsible corporation', and bring about new conditions for corporate communication?
Media analysis	How are media shaped? How do they suggest a specific potential for formation?	In what way does the politicisation of the organisation mean that the organisation is no longer only supposed to form the medium of money, but is also expected to form a number of other communicative media such as power, information and morals? In what way does this change the conditions of the organisation from homophony to polyphony?

Note

[1] However, it is debatable whether Luhmann consistently maintains this strategy, since he, on several occasions, ascribes to semantics a more constitutive role in relation to systems formation (see Stahäli, 1998).

5

A hall of mirrors or a pool of analytical strategies

I n this concluding chapter, I will seek to let the different analytics and analytical strategies in Foucault, Koselleck, Laclau and Luhmann reflect each other and, in so doing, attempt to compare them directly. This requires some form of standard of comparison – a uniform concept that will allow the distinctions to stand out. However, that in itself is a questionable operation, since the principal distinctions that define their constituent diversity are lost in such an endeavour. Nevertheless, this will not restrain me from proceeding to define a kind of 'comprehensive view', the advantage of which is that it paves the way for many fruitful discussions about how it is different to establish, for example, a link to the discourse analysis of Foucault or Laclau respectively.

As already noted, there is no natural universal standard of comparison. The four gentlemen do not ask to be compared and neither do they require a particular standard of reference. However, using Luhmann's ideas, I have chosen to construct a concept of analytical strategy on which I will base my comparisons of the four writers. This will, of course, have the effect of making the others appear in a Luhmannian light, but there are reasons for my choice of perspective. The two principal reasons are width and level of abstraction. First, in my opinion, Luhmann possesses the greatest potential of inclusion due to his rather general but also highly potent theory of second-order observations. Second, Luhmann's concepts appear to permit the development of a productive concept of analytical strategy. The first part of the conclusion will therefore offer this as a standard of comparison.

Conditions of comparisons of discourse theories and systems theories

The basis of comparison is a specific notion of analytical strategy, which is founded on the theory of second-order observations. Analytical strategy can be viewed as a second-order strategy for the observation of how the social emerges in observations (or enunciations and articulations). The elaboration of an analytical strategy involves the shaping of a specific gaze that allows for the environment to appear as consisting of the observations of other people.

Precondition 1

The first precondition of this idea of analytical strategy is that an observation is an indication within the scope of a *distinction*, meaning that it is the distinction that divides the world into observer and observed, thus making the environment appear in a specific way.

Precondition 2

Systems theory, conceptual history and discourse analyses are all, in some sense, analyses of the *second order*: observations of observation, descriptions of description, conceptualisations of concepts or designations of signs. Only while this condition is maintained is the comparison productive.

Precondition 3

The third precondition is the realisation that, on this second-order level, it does not make much sense to let one's research be guided by rules of method. This is simply because a definition of methodological rules leads to an ontologisation of the social phenomena, when the aim is precisely *de-ontologisation*. The equivalent of methodological rules in second-order observation is analytical strategy. Second-order observation is aware that the world is not asking to be observed in any particular way. Second-order observers perceive of the world as poly-contextual, as dependent on the distinction shaped by observation. Consequently, second-order observers can choose how the world should appear by deciding on a particular way of seeing, by connecting with a particular distinction. This is what analytical strategy is about: choosing a way of seeing and accounting for its implications regarding the way the world appears and does not appear. Observations of observations as observations are contingent in relation to the chosen way of seeing. It is always possible to observe the second order in a different way. A decision has to be made, therefore, and the decision calls for an explanation.

Precondition 4

The elaboration of an analytical strategy consists of four choices:

1. Choice of guiding distinction.
2. Conditioning of guiding distinction.
3. Choice of point of observation.
4. Choice of potential combination of analytical strategies.

Precondition 5

One also needs a guiding distinction, by which I mean the distinction that can define the frame for observations of the second order. The guiding distinction divides the world to the second-order observer and dictates how the world can be observed. The guiding distinction creates the necessary distance between the object and the observer, but also defines which questions can be posed in relation to the object. The guiding distinction is not predefined but must be decided. Whether the distinction system/environment, regularity/ dispersion of statements, or discourse/discoursivity is defined as the guiding distinction is an essential analytical-strategic choice. The guiding distinction steers the observation and frames the choice of different supporting distinctions. For example, if the choice is system/environment, the world is divided into systems and their environment; if one decides on regularity/dispersion, the world is divided into the dispersion of statements and the regularity of this dispersion. And one sees *only* that, which is precisely the purpose of the guiding distinction: to discipline our way of seeing so that we do not involuntarily fall back on first-order observation. This is why Foucault expends so much energy on sharpening his discourse-analytical focus. He knows that he is only able to observe the discourse as it appears if his way of seeing is refined enough to keep him from reducing his discourse analysis to discourse commentary.

Precondition 6

The conditioning of the guiding distinction is the specification of those conditions by which one and not the other side of a distinction can be indicated in a second-order observation. It does not suffice to distinguish between system and environment. One must also define when a system can be perceived as a system, when a system can historically be said still to be the same system, when the system has evolved into a different system and when the system has ceased to be a system. Otherwise the guiding distinction can only obtain the status of a loose metaphor in relation to which an observer's indication of system and environment respectively becomes completely arbitrary. This, of course, applies to all guiding distinctions. We could thus ask:

- When is a discourse a discursive formation? That is, when can we reasonably indicate a discursive formation?
- When does a concept of meaning reach into the future through its condensation?
- When is a nodal point or an anchor point firmly anchored?

Whereas the guiding distinction constitutes the fundamental openness and closure of second-order observation (that is, the conditions of observation emerging as object for observation), the conditioning defines the empirical sensitivity of second-order observation, including the openness of the analysis to criticism. The clearer and more unambiguous the conditioning, the greater the sensitivity of the analytical strategy to the empirical, which amounts to saying that the clearer the conditioning of the guiding distinction, the more evident the falsification criteria of the second-order observation. A discourse analysis without well-defined criteria for the indication of discursive formations immunises itself to tangible empirical criticism, thereby dooming any critical discussion of the analysis to a meta-discussion. (Unfortunately, there are many of these types of discourse analyses.)

Precondition 7

I understand point of observation to be maintained through external reference in a second-order observation. It is not enough to decide on a guiding distinction and to condition it in order to adhere to the analytical eye. As Foucault points out, different statements can be read very differently depending on the discursive regularity one employs. In relation to discourse analysis, the point of observation implies a choice of discursive reference, that is, a definition of the question whose genealogy one wishes to unravel and the implications this has for fixing the point of observation. It is my view that this is, as already mentioned, what Foucault discusses when he, for example, dwells on the criteria for periodisation. Similarly, in systems theory the analysis depends entirely on the systems reference of the second-order observer. Do we perceive of the communication as a system of interaction, an as organisational system or as a social system? Each communication can appear as an event in several systems simultaneously. Thus, the appearance of the communication to the second-order observer relies on the observer's choice of systems reference (that is, which system he decides to observe). Again, communication does not itself call for a particular point of observation; a choice is required, and the choice must be followed by an explanation.

Precondition 8

Finally, analytical strategies can be combined, as, for example, when Laclau combines deconstruction and hegemonic analysis. Here, a thorough account of the complementation of the analytical strategies is critical.

• What are the rules for joining the different guiding distinctions?

Various discourse and systems theories are comparable on the level of their analytical-strategic potential, that is, on the level of their pool of guiding distinctions, conditionings and points of observation.

Table 5.1: Analytical strategies compared

Analytical strategy	Guiding distinction	Question
Foucault		
Archaeological discourse analysis	Regularity/dispersion of statements	Why did this and no other statement occur in this place?
Genealogy	Continuity/discontinuity	How are different discursive formations and discursive strategies shaped and transformed?
Self-technology analysis	Subjectivation/subjecting	How have self-technologies been created and in what way do they prescribe the way an individual can give itself to itself?
Dispositive analysis	Apparatus/strategic logic	How are forms linked together as functional elements in an apparatus?
	Strategic logic/apparatus	How are discursive or technical elements generalised in a schematic, which creates a strategic logic?
Koselleck		
History of concepts	Meaning/meaning condensed into concepts	How is meaning condensed into concepts, which constitute the space of possibility of the semantic conflicts?
Semantic field analysis	Concept/counter-concept (generality/singularity)	How do concepts appear in relation to their counter-concepts?
		How are temporal (past/future), spatial (outside/inside), and social (us/them) relations produced?
		How are general positions established and how is the general singularised?
Laclau		
Hegemonic analysis	Discourse/discoursivity	How are discourses established in never-concluded battles about fixing floating elements of signification?
Deconstructivist analysis	Signifier/signified	Which infinite logic is installed by the duality in question?
Luhmann		
Form analysis	Unity/difference	What is the unity of the distinction? And which paradox does it establish?
Systems analysis	System/environment	How does a system of communication come into being in a distinction between system and environment?
		How is the system's boundary of meaning and autopoiesis defined?
Differentiation analysis	Similarity/dissimilarity	How are systems differentiated?
		What is the similarity in the dissimilarities of the systems?
		What are the conditions, therefore, of the formation of new systems of communication?
Semantic analysis	Condensation/meaning	How is meaning condensed?
		How does it create a pool of forms, that is, stable and partially general distinctions available to the systems of communication?
Media analysis	Media/form	How are media shaped and how do they suggest a specific potential for formation?
	Form/medium	How are specific media imprinted in concrete forms, thus colouring communication in a particular way?

System and discourse aligned: guiding distinction

Table 5.1 outlines a comparison of Foucault, Koselleck, Laclau and Luhmann in regard to their analytical strategies. The table concerns the analytics drawn out by the different theories, the guiding lines that constitute the analytics and the questions that these guiding lines offer the present research agenda.

Foucault

In Foucault I have isolated four analytics:

- archaeological discourse analysis;
- genealogy;
- self-technology analysis;
- dispositive analysis.

Archaeological discourse analysis

The guiding distinction in archaeological discourse analysis is regularity/ dispersion of statements and it poses the question of why this and no other statement appears in a particular place. Archaeological analysis divides the world into regularity and dispersion, where no regularity can exist without dispersion, since regularity consists of nothing other than the regularity of the dispersion. With this guiding distinction, Foucault allows for analyses of the order of statements without turning the analytical operation into a reductive operation (seeking to reduce, for example, many discursive events to one or few causes and many discursive manifestations to one latent structure), but rather possessing the ability to sustain the statements in their appearance.

Geneaology

The guiding distinction in the genealogical analytical strategy is continuity/ discontinuity, where continuity (that is, the similar or identical) can be continuous only in relation to the discontinuous (that is, the dissimilar or different) and vice versa. This guiding principle allows for questions about the way discursive formations and practices are shaped and transformed. With this guiding distinction, Foucault lets his analysis be sensitive to any statement and any practice that presents itself as new (that is, as freed of prior misconceptions) or as unique (that is, as identical to its origins). The guiding distinction continuity/discontinuity provides Foucault with an analytical strategy that is not easily captured by the stories told by the present of the present but which, in turn, can function as counter-memory.

Self-technology analysis

The guiding difference of self-technology analysis is subjectivation/subjection, which opens up an inquiry into the way the subject is proclaimed as self-proclaimer, the way self-technologies are created and how they prescribe self-activity through which the individual can give itself to itself.

Dispositive analysis

Finally, the guiding difference of dispositive analysis is strategic logic/apparatus but also apparatus/strategic logic. This allows for inquiries into the way discursive or technical elements are generalised within a schematic that brings about a strategic logic and inquiries into how forms are linked together as functional elements in an apparatus through the unfolding of the strategic logic. Dispositive analysis should be viewed as an extension of Foucault's other analytical strategies, since the dispositive analysis inquires about the mutual ordering of those orders addressed by the other analysis.

Koselleck

In the works of Koselleck we seem to find a distinction between two analytical strategies:

- history of concepts, which is diachronic;
- semantic field analysis, which is synchronous.

History of concepts

The concept-historical analytical strategy is, like Foucault's archaeology, of the second order. It is a strategy for the study of the origins of the linguistic space of possibilities. But the guiding distinction and hence the opening question is different. Therefore, although they both work with linguistic units, they are objectified in different ways. Koselleck's diachronic guiding distinction is meaning/meaning condensed into concepts. Koselleck studies the way the creation of meaning is concentrated and contained in concepts that then become carriers of a multitude of meaning, which can organise the shaping of identities and fields of conflict, and thereby extend into the future. The focus is on concepts, which creates different analytical material to that of Foucault's. Whereas Foucault ideally reads everything, Koselleck focuses on what he calls nurtured semantics, that is, writings that have been worked through linguistically and thus employ concepts prudently.

Sematic field analysis

Koselleck's synchronous guiding distinction is concept/counter-concept. This guiding distinction allows for questions about how concepts always emerge within a semantic field in relation to their counter-concept. For example, Koselleck points to the fact that 'us' is always constructed to the exclusion of 'them'; that the present is always established in the tension between space of experience and horizon of meaning; and that any community organises itself internally through the conceptual opposition of up/down.

Laclau

In Laclau we are able to distinguish:

- hegemonic analysis;
- deconstructivist analysis.

Hegemonic analysis

The former analysis corresponds to the history of concepts and archaeological discourse analysis insofar as it aims to study the origins of discourses, but, again, its guiding distinction is different, which means that the question of discourse presents itself differently. The guiding distinction of the analysis of hegemony is discoursivity/discourse. The shaping of discourses is therefore always studied in its capacity to fix the floating elements of discoursivity. Unlike in Foucault's work, the object is not statements in their appearance, but discursive elements that appear relationally and include practice as well as utterances. In a sense, Laclau's hegemonic analysis is closer to Koselleck's history of concepts than it is to Foucault's discourse analysis, because they both emphasise ambiguity and the incessant floating of meaning as that which establishes the political.

Deconstructivist analysis

Conversely, the deconstructive analytical strategy finds no equivalence in Foucault and Koselleck. The deconstructive eye makes an object of the individual differentiation in order to examine the logic that the distinction or duality might install in the discourse. Through deconstruction, we are able to unveil particular mechanisms of the creation of meaning, which operate as a game of dominance between the two sides of the distinction. The combination in Laclau of the two analytical strategies, by defining deconstructed dualities as guiding distinctions in the hegemonic analysis, gives a very different result to a concept-historical or an archaeological discourse analysis.

Luhmann

For Luhmann it becomes difficult to maintain a comprehensive view of the pool of guiding distinctions and the potential combinations. I believe I can define five different analytical strategies in Luhmann:

- form analysis;
- systems analysis;
- differentiation analysis;
- semantic analysis;
- media analysis.

Form analysis

Form analysis bears close resemblance to Laclau's deconstructive analytical strategy, as it concerns the logic of the creation of meaning (identical to paradox in Luhmann), which is installed with specific distinctions. The guiding distinction of form analysis is unity/difference and identifies forms of observation as object by means of this distinction. Form analysis inquires about the distinction that controls observation and about the paradoxes established by the distinction. Form analysis asks about the unity of the separated. In Luhmann, form analysis is never a goal in itself but rather a strategy for the formulation of further questions – primarily the question of how social systems de-paradoxify the very paradoxes on which they are built through communicative operations.

Systems analysis

The guiding distinction for systems analysis is system/environment. With this guiding distinction, the world is divided into system and environment, with system the operative side. It is therefore from the side of the system that the boundary system/environment is defined. In this perspective, communication is always communication within a system, and the boundary system/environment is a boundary of meaning that determines that the creation of meaning in terms of communication happening on different terms outside the system than inside it. The guiding distinction system/environment poses the question of how a system of communication comes into being in the communicative distinction between system and environment.

- How is the boundary of meaning defined in the system and what are the implications for the continuance of the communication in the system?
- In what way is it closed around itself?
- How does it develop a sensitivity to the environment, that is, how does the system define the relevance of the environment?

There is no equivalent to the guiding distinction system/environment in the other programmes for observation. The closest comparison is Foucault's occasional descriptions of the individual discursive formations as regimes of knowledge and truth ascribing a self to discursive formations. In fact, these descriptions exceed Foucault's analytical strategy and its intention to describe discursive formations as the regularity of the irregular. In Koselleck, the closest notion is in the counter-concept us/them, but here we operate exclusively on a semantic level and not on an operative level as with Luhmann's concept of systems.

Differentation analysis

Differentiation analysis employs the guiding distinction similarity/dissimilarity. It can be argued that this is not an independent analytical strategy but rather a supplement to systems analysis, since the guiding distinction similarity/ dissimilarity presupposes the distinction system/environment. However, the guiding distinction similarity/dissimilarity poses questions that are not directly accessible with the guiding distinction system/environment:

- How are systems differentiated?
- What is the similarity in the dissimilarities of the systems?
- What, consequently, are the conditions of the formation of new systems of communication?

With the guiding distinction similarity/dissimilarity, we can observe the similarities defined by the systems of communication in the differences between themselves and their environment. Thus, we can inquire about the similarities in how systems distinguish themselves from each other. In a certain sense, therefore, differentiation analysis is also form analysis because it concerns forms of differentiation, that is, the unity of the dissimilarity of the systems. The closest analogy in the other programmes for observation is probably the strategic level of Foucault's archaeological discourse analysis. Here, he strives to formulate the question of the mutual exclusion of the discursive formations. Nevertheless, the question is not greatly elaborated on the theoretical level by Foucault, but is unfolded in a number of empirical analyses, for example of the epistemic basis of discursive formations (for example Foucault, 1974, 1986a).

Sematic analysis

Semantic analysis uses the guiding distinction meaning/condensed meaning. Semantic analytical strategy asks the questions:

- How is meaning condensed?
- How does meaning establish a pool of forms, that is, stable and partially generalised distinctions available to systems of communication?

Luhmann's semantic analytical strategy is largely inspired by Koselleck's conceptual history, but differs fundamentally through its origins in the concept of system. This is critical to the analytical strategy because it can then be linked with a social theory.

Media analysis

Luhmann's fifth and final analytical strategy uses the guiding distinction form/ medium, where form can only be regarded as such in relation to a medium and vice versa, with form the operative side. Media analysis only finds its equivalent in Foucault's dispositive analysis, in which apparatus corresponds to form and strategic logic corresponds to medium. The strategic logics that Foucault pursued largely resemble Luhmann's symbolically generalised media in their characterisation. Foucault speaks about legal/illegal, Luhmann about right/wrong; Foucault speaks about security preparedness/insecurity and Luhmann speaks about risk/danger. Both medium and strategic logic can only be brought about through something else; that something else is apparatus in Foucault and form in Luhmann. However, Luhmann never ascribes a strategic function to media. The concepts of form and apparatus both constitute the context in which logic and media are inscribed. However, having highlighted the similarities, the big difference is that Foucault's apparatus is a system of relations between forms, whereas Luhmann appears not to have unfolded the potential in the concept of form with respect to the relations of the forms to other forms. (Although he does point to a guiding difference, which he terms element/relation, and one could argue its potential for perspectives similar to those that Foucault opens with his concept of apparatus.) Finally, like dispositive analysis, media analysis constitutes a double movement. It can be approached from the side of the form as well as the side of the medium. We can inquire into the generalisation of a form into a medium, which I call media analysis. But we can also ask which medium is formed by a specific form and with what effects, which I call formation analysis.

Media analysis asks the questions:

- How are media shaped and how do they suggest a particular potential for formation?
- How do media render certain forms of communication probable?

Media analysis allows for analyses of the history of forms of communication:

- How are, for example, language – spoken and written – and media of distribution such as the Internet shaped?
- How do they substantiate entirely new forms of communication?

Moreover, media analysis as a formation analysis creates the possibility of inquiring about existing media available to particular systems of communication, and the potential and limitation of these media in this regard. This includes the way that the formation of specific media in communication (for example, money) implies a communicative closure around a binary value code of having/ not having.

The different guiding distinctions establish strategies for very different observations of the second order. They each pose their set of questions and establish observation as an object in their own way. The guiding distinction not only constructs the object and question, it also implicitly constructs the criteria for shaping concepts and for valid argumentation. A concept's meaning depends on the choice of guiding distinction. It is not possible for a concept to be given the same meaning based on two different guiding distinctions. This applies to a writer's works as well. The concept of 'discourse', for example, is not identical in Laclau's deconstructive strategy and in his analysis of hegemony. In hegemonic analysis, discourse is a structural unity of differences, but such a notion of discourse is inconceivable in deconstructive analytical strategy, in which discourse is the designation of a specific logic linked to a specific duality. I have used names (Foucault, Kossellek, Laclau, Luhmann) as pegs on which to hang analytical strategies, but, in the end, it is not Luhmann who observes but observation itself, framed by a particular distinction, which determines the construction of the object and the criteria for the construction of good arguments and concepts. Depending on the choice of guiding distinction, the concepts are defined in a particular way. This is an object of systematic reflection in Luhmann's conceptual universe.

If one enters via the guiding distinction of semantics (that is, meaning/condensed meaning), the concepts 'system', 'organisation', 'society', 'politics' and 'complexity' appear as various semantics. Thus, we can study the semantic history of, for example, the concept of system, the concept of politics or the concept of complexity. If we enter via the guiding distinction of systems analysis (system/environment), 'system' is not semantics but an autopoietical system of communication, and 'organisation', 'society' and 'politics' are not semantics but different systems of communication. In the same way, the concept of complexity is granted a central theoretical function to the description of the complexity-reducing relation of systems to the environment. If we enter via the guiding distinction of form analysis (indicated/unindicated), the concepts appear as one side of a distinction, for example system contra environment and politics contra non-politics.

In this way, we can continue with all guiding distinctions – Luhmann's as well as the others' – and conduct a systematic examination of what happens to the concepts when a specific distinction is defined as the guiding distinction. All concepts are fundamentally coloured by the choice of guiding distinction, which means that there is no 'true' definition of 'discourse', 'system', 'meaning' and so on, since the criteria for 'true' and 'real' are simply construed through the choice of guiding distinction.

Conditioning and point of observation

Guiding distinctions not only construct questions, object and concepts, they also, as we will now address, establish their own set of analytical-strategic problems and their own questions with a choice of observation point and conditioning guiding distinction. These are questions that can only be solved in relation to the empiricism or reality to which the analytical strategies seek to become sensitive. However, there are certain general aspects regarding the character of these questions within the different analytical strategies. I will attempt to formulate and compare these questions below.

Foucault

Archaeological discourse analysis

Let us, once again, begin with Foucault's archaeological discourse analysis. Here, the fundamental question is the conditioning of the discursive formation. When are we able to identify a discursive formation? The guiding distinction regularity/dispersion of statements is not sensitive to empiricism until it has been established when a regularity in the dispersion of statements constitutes a discursive formation. Without exact criteria for when we can identify regularity and hence discursive formation, our designation of discourses is based solely on intuition (Hebrew for revelation).

In fact, Foucault answers this question thoroughly in his work on knowledge archaeology, but the entire answer depends on which particular form of discourse we are dealing with. There is no guarantee that regularity can signify the same thing at all times and in all discursive contexts. Foucault knows this. As it is, knowledge archaeology precisely designates knowledge as a point of reference. It extends itself into very different areas of knowledge but always in the shape of knowledge. This is evident even down to the level of the specifications by the analytical strategy of the levels of formation, including the emphasis on the object level and the questions of how objects are shaped, placed in hierarchies and classified. We can conceive of numerous other forms of discourses that would not have in common the form of knowledge and would also not, therefore, share the same form of regularity. Hence, knowledge-archaeological analytical strategy possesses an inherent notion of the characteristics of knowledge discourses, but these characteristics themselves become the object of the analysis and discussion of their origins. Accordingly, *The birth of the clinic* (Foucault, 1986b) does not merely concern the history of medical discourse but also the origins of the scientific way of seeing. The conditioning of the guiding distinction is not therefore a question of deciding on a set of premises once and for all. In a discourse analysis, conditioning the concept of discourse is itself an object of analysis. The way a discursive formation is a discursive formation is an intricate part of the discourse analysis. The discursive formation does not, therefore, precede the study of it, since the discursive formation as the subject of discourse analysis can only be demarcated after the completion of the analysis. In practice, this means that the discourse analyst constantly questions the discourse's own criteria for discourse.

Genealogy

In genealogy, the question of conditioning is defined as a question of the measure for the assertion of continuity and discontinuity respectively. However, conditioning in genealogy implies an almost reversed conditioning, since the aim is to criticise predefined notions of continuity and rupture, that is, to criticise the conditioning of continuity and discontinuity through discourses. The aim is an uninterrupted continuation of contingency in relation to continuity and discontinuity. In this respect, genealogy is in strict opposition to archaeology, since genealogy is almost anti-analytical in its rejection of any naturalisation of change. Genealogy is given a Dionysian life-giving function by leaving it open, contrary to the tendency to closure in archaeology due to its propensity for systematism. Incidentally, we can see a parallel here to the function of deconstruction in Laclau in relation to hegemonic analysis and to the function of form analysis in Luhmann in relation to systems analysis.

Self-technology analysis

In self-technology analysis, the central problem of conditioning is the ability to define clearly which form of subjecting applies when. When is a subject expected to give itself to itself? In other words, when is it a matter of subjectivation? The second problem of conditioning concerns when one can speak of technology and self-technology respectively. This problem of conditioning concerns both the question of when to define something as self-technology and the question of which analytical variables we make ourselves sensitive to as analysts. Here, as in knowledge archaeology, Foucault faces the problem of the purist. He would like to let the way self-technology is self-technology remain an empirical, and thus historical, question. However, he needs certain measures that allow him to recognise a self-technology in the first place. The challenge is to apply a concept of self-technology that is as empty as possible and then to imply the conditioning as part of the analytics itself as that which the analysis is fundamentally about. There are, however, four minimum criteria:

1. The transformative form of subjecting.
2. The objectification of the self.
3. Self-directed activity.
4. Telos.

Foucault requires the objectification of the self, requires self-directed activity, and requires that the self-directed activity have a form of telos, but in none of these cases does he specify how this should be done.

Dispositive analysis

Finally, dispositive analysis contains two problems of conditioning. First is the question of when elements are linked in such a way that it is possible to see the emergence of an apparatus. The analysis can leave open which elements have to be present, but one has to be able to define the synchronous cohesion of the elements. As far as I can see, Foucault provides no unambiguous criteria but maintains the argument based on a sense of systematism. Second is the question of when a scheme has obtained the characteristics of a general and strategic logic. Foucault lets the second problem of conditioning depend on the first, since the criterion is that there is not a strategic imperative until it is brought about through an apparatus.

Point of observation

A point of observation must also be decided upon. In Foucault's four analytical strategies, this decision depends on the question one wishes to pose and pursue in the analysis, and choice of question always implies a choice of discursive reference.

For example...

The question might be the birth of the complete employee, but the specification of this question implies a definition of whether the point of observation is a scientific discourse and, if so, which one (for example, psychology or organisational theory). It might also be a political discourse, for example that of administrational politics. Depending on the discourse one chooses as point of observation, different criteria for discourse exist and different articulations and notions of the 'complete employee' appear.

In discourses of organisational studies, the 'complete employee' operates within a specific theoretical programme, which obtains its identity through its differentiation from other theoretical programmes. In discourses of administrative politics, the 'complete employee' does not gain acceptance because of the concept's capacity for organisational description but because of its ability to function as a strategic tool for the commitment of the individual employee to the changes in the public sector. The choice of observation point directs discourse analysis and genealogy in different directions. Moreover, well-defined points of observation allow for studies of interdiscursive relationships, for example in regard to the 'complete employee'.

Koselleck

Concept-historical analysis

In Koselleck's concept-historical analysis the most essential problem of conditioning is defining the criteria for when a concept can be regarded as a concept, which means, in Koselleck, a definition of when meaning has been condensed into the form of the concept. The problem of conditioning is rather unproblematic in Koselleck, since all his concepts are developed with the problem of conditioning in mind. The measures for when a concept is a concept are fairly unambiguous but the entire analysis, in turn, depends on the fact that the creation of meaning possesses exactly these conceptual qualities. This includes the existence of a nurtured semantics in which the concepts can appear as object to the history of concepts. Conceptual history is not able to capture creation of meaning that does not obtain the form of concept (for example, symbols or images).

Semantic field analysis

In Koselleck's semantic field analysis the problem of conditioning is a definition of when a semantic field possesses the characters of a field. The problem of conditioning in regard to semantic fields has not been unfolded thoroughly in Koselleck. However, his notion of the fundamental general distinctions (us/them, inside/outside, past/future and up/down) provides some traceable leads. At the very least, a semantic field must comprise stable (that is, repeated) distinctions of the type mentioned above. Moreover, studies of the specific historical tension between the two sides of the distinctions contribute to the definition of conditions of particular semantic fields.

Point of observation

In Koselleck, defining an observation point concerns the designation of the semantic field to which the history of concepts and the field analysis are linked. As in Foucault's discourse analysis, the semantics to which a concept belongs is not a given: one word can indicate various concepts depending on the reference to a semantic field. A conceptual history of the concept of 'child' extends in many different directions and has many different sources, depending on whether the semantics of education, law or love function as the point of observation.

Laclau

In Laclau we see the emergence of a number of problems of conditioning, which, in some cases, take on more serious dimensions than in the analyses of Foucault and Koselleck. Generally, we might regret that Laclau has abstained from empirical work, since this kind of experience might have influenced his theoretical architecture. However, no efforts have been made towards the conditioning of the apparatus for observation, which means that what appears coherent and consistent within the theory is transformed into rather feeble metaphors on confrontation with an actual object. This applies to the concepts of discourse, and floating and empty signifier. The concept of empty signifier is particularly anti-empirical.

Hegemonic analysis

The first problem of conditioning directly concerns the guiding distinction discoursivity/discourse. On the one hand, Laclau's formulation of a general discourse theory as opposed to Foucault's specific knowledge archaeology implies that it is considerably more open concerning the question of which discourses can be made the object of a discourse analysis. This is a definite strength. On the other hand, however, it offers no guidelines for when we can speak of discourse. The only general measure for such a definition is that a partial fixation of the discourse must occur, but nothing general can be said about when this happens. Any hegemonic analysis thus faces the problem of conditioning the measures for partial fixation.

This is not to be read as a fundamental criticism of Laclau's hegemoic analysis but as a demonstration of the fact that the analyst will not find much guidance for such an operation in Laclau. I have no reservations as to its potency and ability for conditioning the guiding distinction discoursivity/discourse, although I wish to point out that discourse theory as such does not invite such an endeavour. Laclau himself does not indicate this as a problem. Moreover, one might consider whether the assertion of discourse in general does not oppose any attempt to historise (and hence condition) the way that discourse can appear as discourse in different contexts and at different times. Nevertheless, I believe there is one possible extension of the conditioning of the guiding distinction discoursivity/discourse in the combination of hegemonic analysis with deconstruction, in which the logicity of dualites can perhaps provide conditioning measures for discourse by constituting the guiding principles for hegemonic analysis. A discourse of power is thus conditioned by occurring across the distinction power/freedom, and a political discourse by occurring across the distinction particularity/universality and so on.

Whereas it is thus possible, in my opinion, to define measures for partial fixation, I believe that one comes up against fundamental difficulties in relation to a concept such as the empty signifier. The theoretical function of the empty signifier is an indication of the boundaries of meaning (not of one meaning but of 'meaning' as such), and the boundaries of meaning cannot be signified – not even by the discourse analyst. Whereas the empty signifier (of which I am very fond as a theoretical concept) sustains a significant theoretical function, it has no empirical analytical potency. It evades any attempt at conditioning. It is, of course, possible to look for concepts that are 'reasonably' empty (such as ecological sustainability or local community) but then the theoretical status of the concept is lost. It is either empty or not empty. It cannot be half empty, since it does not then indicate the boundaries of meaning but at most the floating character of meaning. This means that the empty signifier, as a result, becomes synonymous with the floating signifier, which is also an empirically potent concept.

Why is it that the empty signifier does not allow for conditioning? In fact, this is not strange at all. The empty signifier does not allow for conditioning because, by defining the boundary of meaning, it simultaneously constitutes the boundary of the discourse analyst insofar as he works within meaning. The empty signifier designates the space from which the discourse is analysed and is therefore unable to be indicated by the discourse analysis itself.

Deconstructivist analysis

The question of conditioning obtains a peculiar role in relation to deconstruction. Deconstruction is precisely not an analysis in the sense of a reductive operation, which means that there is no analysis that needs conditioning. Of course, one can maintain that the choice of duality represents a significant choice. It seems reasonable to ask: Why deconstruction of this particular distinction? Why, for one thing, is freedom defined in opposition to power? Why tolerance in opposition to intolerance? Which other oppositions could be deconstructed? But the answer to the question of why it is this particular distinction can only be given in hegemonic analysis. In the analysis of hegemony where the duality is transformed into a guiding principle, the way, scope and effects by which a specific distinction manifests itself become evident. It is not until this point that the question of the duality and the generality, and the historical-empirical status of its associated logic, is conditioned.

Point of observation

In Laclau the choice of observation point concerns, as in Foucault, the choice of discursive reference. Moreover, the choice of a specific duality and logic affects the point of observation. The 'same' discursive formation appears significantly different depending on the deconstructed duality one defines as guiding principle, that is, which logic the hegemonies are seen as constellations of. The movement discoursivity ⟶ discourse happens differently in, for example, the logic of signification, the logic of representation and the logic of universalisation. If the chosen guiding principle is the logic of representation, the movement appears as a description of how different relationships between representative and represented are articulated and fixed. If, on the other hand, the guiding principle is the logic of universalisation, hegemonic analysis becomes a description of how the relationship between the universal and the particular is articulated and fixed, including how particular positions are sought, universalised and granted the authority to define the boundaries for the appearance of particularity.

Luhmann

Form analysis

The problem of conditioning in Luhmann's form analysis has the same qualities as the problem of conditioning in relation to deconstruction in Laclau. As we have seen, form analysis concerns the unity of the distinction, hence, the primary task is to recognise which distinction is the object of the form analysis. The first difficulty is therefore in a motivation of the other side of the distinction in relation to the indication one seeks to observe.

For example...

If one focuses on risk, the question is:

- What does the other side of risk consist of?

In his form analysis of risk communication, Luhmann chooses to replace the opposition risk/security by the opposition risk/danger. The question is therefore:

- Why is danger the other side of the distinction to risk?

As was the case with deconstruction, the question cannot be answered until form analysis functions as input for another analysis, for example a semantic analysis or a systems analysis, in which the unfolding of the paradoxical character of form can be studied. Only in studies of the de-paradoxification of paradoxes will it become evident to what degree and with what implications a form manifests itself. Only through de-paradoxification can we follow form in its chains of distinctions and only then can we determine to what extent communication follows a specific form.

Systems analysis

I have already touched upon the problem of conditioning in systems analysis where the guiding distinction is system/environment. The questions are:

- When can we say that communication forms an autopoietical system?
- When is the system identical with itself and when has it developed into a new system?

Differentiation analysis

In Luhmann's differentiation analysis, the problem of conditioning pertains to the measures of similarity in a distinction to be pinpointed as a form of differentiation.

- When are systems equal in their way of defining themselves in relation to the environment?
- Moreover, what allows for the description of a specific form of differentiation to draw conclusions in respect of the possibilities of continued systems formation?

Evidently, all social systems do not adhere to the same form of differentiation. Luhmann claims that functional differentiation is presently the primary form of differentiation, but this does not mean that systems adhering to a different form of differentiation are not continually formed (for example, biker gangs that define themselves in accordance with codes of honour, or systems that regulate membership based on ethnicity, or family systems that still present themselves as patriarchal dynasties). The enunciative power depends entirely on how demanding one conditions the analysis.

Media analysis

Finally, the problem of conditioning in Luhmann's media analysis concerns the measures for the designation of a new medium. As previously noted, a medium is always a medium in relation to a form, but the tension between form and medium varies historically. Consequently, we cannot presuppose deductive measures for media, since this would exclude from the analysis the historical character of the media. For example, the ways in which language, radio, television and money create media are very different. Gradually, Luhmann has constructed a distinction between types of media:

* language;
* media of distribution;
* general symbolic media.

Evidently, each of the types holds definitional measures but, at the same time, each medium typically exceeds the general definition. The media never completely function as media in exactly the same way, and it is therefore critical to the empirical sensitivity of the analysis that the conditioning possesses an inductive rather than a deductive character. Parallel to Foucault's discourse analyses, we cannot predefine a final conditioning of the point at which a medium can be regarded as a medium. The conditioning happens as part of the analysis in which the demands on the chosen medium are gradually intensified, and in which this evolution makes the object appear increasingly clear and causes the analysis to heighten its sensitivity to empirical details. The analysis can be seen as completed once one has reached a delimitation of the characteristics of the medium as medium. As with archaeological discourse analysis, the object (that is, the specific discursive formation) cannot therefore be presupposed. On the contrary, the object is the result of the analysis, including the measures for the assertion of the object.

Semantic analysis

The problem of conditioning in Luhmann's semantic analysis has the same definitions as in Koselleck's history of concepts in as much as Luhmann has found considerable inspiration here. I will therefore not elaborate any further on this point, except to say that the fundamental question is:

* When is meaning condensed and when does a semantic rupture exist?

Point of observation

The question of choice of observation point in systems theory always involves, as a minimum, a choice of systems reference. Any communication can exist as an event in numerous systems of communication. At the very least, one must indicate whether the point of reference of the analysis is a system of interaction, an organisational system or a social system. However, as we have seen in Chapter Four on Luhmann, systems have the capacity to differentiate themselves into sub-systems where the sub-systems define their own environment and where the 'master'-system is observed as the environment of the sub-system. It is always possible to shift the point of observation and, in so doing, the observed communications emerge in new ways. It is always possible to move back in the systems differentiation so that what used to be system now appears as sub-system, or forward in the differentiation so that what used to be system now appears as environment. Regardless of the analytical strategy one connects with, one cannot evade, in Luhmann's systems theory, the indication of a systems reference. In this way, the guiding distinction system/environment obtains a special status in relation to the other guiding distinctions, as it somehow arranges the relationships between the analyses.

In addition to the choice of systems reference, other questions regarding the definition of observation point can be formulated depending on the analytical strategy.

Combining analytical strategies

I have tried to describe Foucault, Koselleck, Laclau and Luhmann as analytical strategists. I have grouped their writings under the heading of one umbrella by defining their work as different theoretical programmes for the observation of the second order. I have suggested and prescribed to them a particular notion of analytical strategy based on a distinction between guiding distinction, conditioning and point of observation. Now the question is this: Are we free to cross-combine these analytical strategies? It is one thing to compare and to allow for the programmes to reflect each other; it is something else to observe the programmes as a pool of analytical strategies between which one is reasonably free to choose and across which elements can be transferred and combined.

I do not have the ultimate answer to this question. Fundamentally, however, we should remind ourselves that the four programmes have themselves been pieced together and are made up of fragments from very contradictory theories. Considering the fact that Luhmann is able to fuse elements from theories as distinct as Bateson's theory of information, Husserl's phenomenology, Parson's systems theory and Spencer-Brown's form calculus, why should we not feel free to import elements from Laclau's hegemonic analysis into Luhmann's analysis of semantics? When Laclau takes the liberty of bringing together elements from Foucault's discourse analysis with elements from Lacan's psychoanalysis, despite Foucault's dislike for Lacan's work, why should we not consider the combinatory constellation of systems analysis and hegemonic analysis?

Table 5.2: Problems of conditioning related to the analytical strategies

Analytical strategy	Problems of conditioning	Fixation of point of observation
Foucault		
Archaeological discourse analysis	When can we speak of 'regularity'?	Which discursive problem is pursued?
	When can a statement be regarded as a statement?	What is the discursive reference?
Genealogy	What are the measures for the identification of continuity and discontinuity respectively?	What is the discursive reference?
Self-technology analysis	When can we speak of subjectivation?	What is the discursive reference?
	When can something be regarded as technology?	What is the discursive reference?
Dispositive analysis	When are the elements sufficiently connected for them to be called an apparatus?	What is the discursive reference?
	When is a schematic a general and strategic logic?	What is the discursive reference?
Koselleck		
History of concepts	When is meaning condensed?	Which semantic field is referred to?
Semantic field analysis	When does a semantic field possess the qualities of a field?	What is the discursive reference?
Laclau		
Hegemonic analysis	Which conditions must be met for someone to speak of discourse?	What is the discursive reference?
		Which logic is defined as guiding principle?
Deconstructivist analysis	Why this particular distinction?	Which discursive problem is pursued?
Luhmann		
Form analysis	Why this particular distinction?	What is the systems reference?
	Why this particular 'other side' of the distinction?	Which form is defined as the guiding principle?
Differentiation analysis	What are the measures for a similarity in a distinction to be designated as a form of differentiation?	Which form is defined as the guiding principle?
Semantic analysis	When is meaning condensed?	Which form is defined as the guiding principle?
	When does a semantic rupture exist?	
Media analysis	What are the measures for the recognition of a medium?	Which form is defined as the guiding principle?

Luhmann and Foucault have both posited the non-existence of a 'better' strategy. Foucault has consciously striven not to form a school – from Foucault's perspective, 'Foucault' is not a valid argument for a particular analytical strategy. In the words of Luhmann: 'A choice of guiding distinction is precisely a choice!' There is no transcendental space from which a specific choice of guiding distinction can be substantiated in opposition to a different choice. Moreover, the empirical also does not ask to be observed in any particular way.

In the end, I believe that one should not let the works impede the development of new analytical strategies. Basically, the guiding distinction is what guides the observation, not Foucault, Laclau, Koselleck or Luhmann. What *is* important, therefore, are the existing and potential relationships between the analytical strategies one might choose to bring together and the thorough reflection of how the choice of guiding distinction defines the measures for other concepts and for their application. This includes the introduction of any 'foreign' concepts.

Evidently, if one does decide to combine (which I have done on several occasions, for example in Andersen, 1995), certain problems occur.

First, it is not possible to simultaneously employ more than one guiding distinction without causing the perspective to become unstable and to oscillate uncontrollably between the different guiding distinctions. One analysis cannot be linked to both the guiding distinction discoursivity/discourse as well as system/environment. One might use the two guiding distinctions to define a combinatory analytical strategy, in which one contemplates two separate analyses that somehow supplement each other. This requires an account of the complementarity of the two strategies and the ability to tailor the concepts in such a way that they are precisely complementary and not competing and conflicting.

Second, if one imports elements from one analytical strategy into another, these elements need to be redefined in respect to the guiding distinction. If, for example, Laclau's 'nodal point' is brought into Luhmann's semantic analysis, it must be decided which specific analytical strategic status the concept might obtain there (if any!). One must answer the question: Which function does the concept serve in the overall analytical strategy?

I personally have found it a natural progression to introduce elements of Foucault's archaeology into a Luhmannian historical-semantic analysis. In fact, I have simply used a number of Foucault's discourse-analytical variables in order to operationalise the fact dimension in Luhmann's semantics (Andersen and Born, 2000).

Third, the combination of analytical strategies affects the separate analytical strategies, for example, by demands on their conditioning. When semantic analysis is combined with differentiation analysis in Luhmann, it is required that the conditioning of the two analytical strategies be congenial, so that the correlation between a rupture in the semantic evolution can be related to displacements in the form of differentiation. Evidently, the difficulties of a complementary linking of different analytical strategies do not diminish when working across the different programmes of observation.

> **For example...**
>
> The combination of Foucault's archaeological discourse analysis with Luhmann's systems analysis implicates the problem that Foucault does not employ a distinction between system and semantics. On the contrary, Foucault's analyses sometimes operate almost as systems possessing a self, for example in descriptions of discursive conflicts. At the very least, a combination of these two analytical strategies must involve a solution to this problem, for example by weeding out the systemic elements of the concept of discourse in order to avoid the simultaneous application of two different concepts of system. Of course, one might object that it is then no longer a Foucauldian knowledge archaeology but, the question is whether that difference makes a difference.

Future questions

A second-order perspective does not form a contrast to empirical imminence. Stepping back and inquiring *about* the categories and not *from* the categories, about the semantics and discourses, and not from the semantics and discourses, about the systems and not from the systems does not mean a decreased level of concretion or a greater distance to empirical matters. On the contrary, the indiscriminate use of preconceived categories and methods of first-order observations creates immunity from the empirical. Only through the discussion of the way we discuss are we able to regain sensitivity to the empirical and avoid automatic social descriptions such as, for example, the aforementioned discourse on the restriction of the freedom of nations in relation to European integration (in the Introduction). However, as demonstrated above, a wealth of analytical-strategic difficulties follow from the shift from a first-order perspective to a second-order perspective where observation is observed as observations. Only through a dedicated approach to the analytical-strategic problems is it possible for a second-order perspective to make the empirical pose a challenge to the observation.

In this book, I have tried to encourage an analytical-strategic discussion across a range of different epistemologies based on the idea that they might at least inform each other in respect to the elaboration of analytical-strategic problems.

As regards Laclau and Luhmann at least, there exists no tradition for analytical-strategic discussions. Laclau has never undertaken any empirical work and, although Luhmann has conducted plenty of empirical work, his students appear to be primarily interested in his theoretical endeavours. It is my opinion, however, that there is no point in developing discourse-analytical manifestos or systems-theoretical concepts without directing these to an object. A second-order observation is not worth attention unless it is an observation of specific empirical observations. Within the environments that refer to Foucault, Luhmann, Laclau and others, we find an anti-methodological sentiment. This

Figure 5.1: Analytical strategy

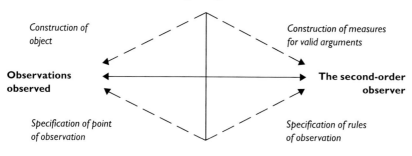

Choice of guiding distinction

Construction of
object

Construction of measures
for valid arguments

**Observations
observed**

**The second-order
observer**

Specification of point
of observation

Specification of rules
of observation

Choice of conditioning

is completely understandable. What I am trying to point out is that method is not the only way in which one can approach the relationship between theory and empiricism. It is possible to install analytical strategy in the place of method in an epistemologically founded second-order observation, and hence discuss problems of operationalisation, without finding oneself with ontologising rules of method.

In Figure 5.1 I have tried to illustrate my suggestions for a concept of analytical strategy.

The choice of guiding distinction divides the world into the second-order observer and his object, the observed observation. Neither observer nor object is predefined. They are both construed through the choice of guiding distinction. They are internal analytical-strategic constructions. The guiding distinction defines the measures for anything to be observable as object while simultaneously constructing the criteria, which the observer must employ in argumentation and formation of concepts. The definition of a good and valid argument, thus, is an internal analytical-strategic construction.

Subsequently, the choice of conditioning is the specification of object and observation respectively. Throughout this book, the former has been designated 'the specification of point of observation', that is, the question of which specific discourse, system or observation the second-order observer lays claim to in his observation. The latter is that which I have generally termed 'conditioning of guiding distinction', which concerns the specification of rules for observation as regards the indication of one or the other side of the guiding distinction (for example, the specification of when a discourse is a discourse).

Consequently, one cannot refer to any external authority when dealing with analytical-strategic questions. In this book, I have posed what I consider some of the key analytical-strategic questions. However, other questions can be asked, concerning for example sources, text and text analysis, and the integration of traditional methods in epistemological analytical strategies. I suppose my claim is that, no matter which question one asks, it must possess the possibility of reformulation *within* the concept of analytical strategy stated above.

In conclusion, I will provide, as an example, the question of sources.

For example...

- What is a 'source' in an epistemological observation and hence what are the conditions of criticism of the sources?

This question entails two analytical-strategic questions. First, the construction of sources is a question regarding the choice of guiding distinction and, second, criticism of sources becomes a question of conditioning. What is regarded as a source in an epistemological observation is naturally an internal construction in the analytical strategy in the same way that the object is a construction. There are no predefined sources 'out there'. Sources are constructed as a tool in an analytical strategy to obtain empirical sensitivity. Thus, the construction of something as a source is an analytical-strategic choice concerning the empirical sensitivity one wishes to attain in relation to the internally constructed object.

Subsequently, criticism of sources becomes a question of the specification of the rules for observation. One example could be Foucault's knowledge-archaeological strategy with the guiding distinction regularity/dispersion of statements. Based on this guiding distinction, Foucault constructs sources as monuments in a discourse. A discourse-analytical monument is a pivot in discourse, something that stands out and indicates a difference in the discursive regularity. As monument, the source is therefore anything but a document. It documents nothing. In Foucault, the monument is not a source of information. The source constructed as monument is simply a discursive injection. Foucault has not explicitly developed a 'criticism of monuments', but such a criticism would consist in the specification of rules for when a monument can be regarded as monument, that is, when we can say that a specific text or image embodies the injection of a specific discourse (Andersen, 1994).

References

Althusser, L. and Balibar, E. (1970) *Reading capital*, London: NLB.

Andersen, N.Å. (1994) 'Institutionel historie', *COS-rapport*, Copenhagen: Copenhagen Business School.

Andersen, N.Å. (1995) *Selvskabt forvaltning*, Copenhagen: Nyt fra Samfundsvidenskaberne.

Andersen, N.Å. (1996) *Udlicitering – når det private bliver politisk*, Copenhagen: Nyt fra Samfundsvidenskaberne.

Andersen, N.Å. (1997) *Udlicitering – strategi og historie*, Copenhagen: Nyt fra Samfundsvidenskaberne.

Andersen, N.Å. and Born, A. (2000) 'Complexity and change: two "semantic tricks" in the triumphant oscillating organization', *System Practice and Action Research*, vol 13, no 3.

Andersen, N.Å. and Born, A. (2001) *Kærlighed og omstilling – italesættelsen af den offentligt ansatte*, Copenhagen: Nyt fra Samfundsvidenskaberne.

Balibar, E. (1994) 'Subjection and subjectivation', in J. Copjec (ed) *Supposing the subject*, London: Verso.

Baraldi, C., Corsi G. and Esposito, E. (1997) *GLU, Glossar zu Niklas Luhmanns Theorie sozialer Systeme*, Frankfurt am Main: Suhrkamp.

Barthes, R. (1990) S/Z, Oxford: Blackwell Publishers.

Beronius, M. (1991) *Genealogi och Sociologi*, Kunghult: Brutus Östlings Bokförlag Symposion AB.

Bornmann, L. (1998) 'Glossar zu Niklas Luhmanns Theorie sozialer Systeme', at http://www.uni-kassel.de/~bornmann/luhmann.htm.

Bourdieu, P. (1992) *Language and symbolic power*, Cambridge: Polity Press.

Brenner, N. (1994) 'Foucault's new functionalism', *Theory and Society*, no 23, pp 679-709.

Brunner, O., Conze, W. and Koselleck, R. (1972) *Geschichtliche Grundbegriffe, historisches Lexikon zur politisch-sozialen Sprache in Deutschland*, vol 1, Stuttgart: Klett-Gotta.

Chouliaraki, L. and Fairclough, N. (1999) *Discourse in late modernity: Rethinking critical discourse analysis,* Edinburgh: Edinburgh University Press.

Dahlager, L. (2001) 'I forebyggelsen magt', *Distinktion*, no 3, pp 91-102.

Davidson, A.I. (1986) 'Archaeology, genealogy, ethics', in D.C. Hoy (ed) *Foucault: A critical reader*, Oxford: Basil Blackwell.

de Certeau, M. (1975) *Spor af historien*, Copenhagen: Vinten.

de Saussure, F. (1990) *Course in general linguistics*, London: Duckworth.

Dean, M. (1994) 'A social structure of many souls: moral regulation, government and self-formation', *The Canadian Journal of Sociology*, vol 19, no 2, pp 145-68.

Dean, M. (1998) 'Administrativ Ascetism', in M. Dean and B. Hindess, *Governing Australia*, Cambridge: Cambridge University Press.

Dean, M. (1999) *Governmentality*, London: Sage Publications.

Deleuze, G. (1992) 'What is a dispositif?', in T.J. Armstrong (ed) *Michel Foucault philosopher*, London: Harvester Wheatsheaf.

Derrida, J. (1976) 'Structure, sign and play in the discourse of the human sciences', in J. Derrida, *Writing and difference*, Chicago, IL: University of Chicago Press.

Derrida, J. (1980) *Of grammatology*, Baltimore, NJ: Johns Hopkins University Press.

Derrida, J. (1988) 'Letter to a Japanese friend', in D. Wood and R. Bernasconi (eds) *Derrida and différance*, Chicago, IL: Northwestern University Press.

Descombes, V. (1980) *Modern French philosophy*, Cambridge: Cambridge University Press.

Esposito, E. (1996) 'From self-reference to autology: how to operationalize a circular approach', *Social Science Information*, pp 269-81.

Fairclough, N. (1992) *Discourse and social change*, Cambridge: Polity Press.

Fairclough, N. (1995) *Critical discourse analysis*, London: Longman.

Foucault, M. (1970) 'Diskurs og Diskontinuitet' in P. Madsen (ed) *Strukturalisme*, Copenhagen: Rhodos, p 152 (the article is a translation into Danish of sections 1 and 2 of Foucault, M. [1968] 'Réponse au cercle d'épistémologie', *Cahiers pour l'analyse*, vol 9).

Foucault, M. (1971) *Madness and civilization*, London: Routledge.

Foucault, M. (1972) 'The discourse on language', in M. Foucault, *The archaeology of knowledge*, New York, NY: Pantheon Books.

Foucault, M. (1974) *The order of things*, London: Routledge.

Foucault, M. (1976) *Mental illness and psychology*, Berkeley and Los Angeles, CA: University of California Press.

Foucault, M. (1977) *Discipline and punish*, London: Penguin.

Foucault, M. (1978) *The history of sexuality, Volume 1*, London: Penguin.

Foucault, M. (1980) 'The confession of the flesh: a conversation', in C. Gordon (ed) *Power/knowledge, selected interviews and other writings, Michel Foucault*, New York, NY: Pantheon Books.

Foucault, M. (1986a) *The archaeology of knowledge*, London: Tavistock.

Foucault, M. (1986b) *The birth of the clinic*, London: Routledge.

Foucault, M. (1991) 'Nietzsche, genealogy, history', in P. Rabinow (ed) *The Foucault reader*, London: Penguin.

Foucault, M. (1997) *Essential works of Foucault, 1959-1989, Volume 1: Ethics, subjectivity of truth*, New York, NY: New York Press.

Foucault, M. (1998a) *Essential works of Foucault 1954-1984, Volume 2: Aesthetics, method, and epistemology*, New York, NY: New York Press.

Foucault, M. (1998b) 'The political technology of individuals', in L.H. Martin, H. Gutman and P.H. Hutton (eds) *Technologies of the self: A seminar with Michel Foucault*, Amhurst, MA: University of Massachusetts Press.

Günther, G. (1976) *Beiträge zur Grundlegung einer operationsfähigen Dialectic*, Hamburg: Felix Meiner Verlag.

Habermas, J. (1972) *Knowledge and human interests*, London: Polity Press.

Habermas, J. (1991) *Communication and the evolution of society*, London: Polity Press.

Habermas, J. (1992) *Moral consciousness and communicative action*, London: MIT Press.

Habermas, J. (1996) *Between facts and norms: Contribution to a discourse theory of law and democracy*, Cambridge: Polity Press.

Hacking, I. (1986) 'Self-improvement', in D.C. Hoy (eds) *Foucault: A critical reader*, Oxford: Basil Blackwell.

Heidegger, M, (1978) *Being and time*, London: Blackwell Publishers.

Ifversen, J. (1997) 'Om magt, demokrati og diskurs', *Begrebshistoriske studier No 2*, Århus: Center for Kulturforskning, Århus Universitet.

Ifversen, J. and Østergård, U. (1996) 'Europæisk Civilisation, begrebshistorie og diskursanalyse', in Østergård og Ifversen (ed) *Begreb og historie*, Århus: Århus Universitet.

Kaufmann, L.H. (1987) 'Self-reference and recursive forms', *Journal of Social and Biological Structures*, vol 10, pp 53-72.

Kent, C.A. (1986) 'Michel Foucault: doing history, or undoing it?', *Canadian Journal of History*, pp 371-95.

Kneer, G. and Nassehi, A. (1993) *Niklas Luhmanns Theorie sozialer Systeme*, München: Wilhem Fink Verlag.

Koselleck, R. (1972) 'Einleitung', in Brunner, Conze and R. Koselleck (eds) *Geschichtliche Grundbegriffe, Historisches Lexikon zur politisch-sozialen Sprache in Deutschland*, vol 1, Stuttgart: Klett-Gotta.

Koselleck, R. (1982) 'Begriffsgeschichte and social history', *Economy and Society*, vol 11, no 4, pp 409-27.

Koselleck, R. (1985) *Futures past: On the semantics of historical time*, Cambridge, MA: MIT Press.

Koselleck, R. (1987) 'Historik und Hermeneutik', in R. Koselleck and H.-G. Gadamer (eds) *Historik und Hemeneutik*, Heidelberg: Carl Winter Universitätsverlag.

Kosselleck, R. (1988) *Critique and crisis*, Oxford: Berg.

Kosselleck, R. (1989) 'Linguistic change and the history of events', *Journal of Modern History*, no 61, pp 649-66.

Krause, D. (1996) *Luhmann-Lexikon*, Stuttgart: Ferdinand Enke Verlag.

Krause-Jensen, E. (1978) *Viden og magt*, Copenhagen: Rhodos.

Kristeva, J. (1989) *Language, the unknown*, London: Prentice Hall/Harvester Wheatsheaf.

Lacan, J. (1982) 'God and the jouissance of the woman: a love letter', in J. Mitchell and J. Rose (eds) *Feminine sexuality*, London: Macmillan.

Lacan, J. (2001) *Ecrits*, London: Routledge.

Laclau, E. (1983) 'Transformations of advanced industrial societies and the theory of the subject', in S. Haenninen and L. Palden (eds) *Rethinking ideology*, Berlin: Argument Verlag, International General.

Laclau, E. (1985) 'Hegemoni – en ny politisk logik', interview in A. Andresen (ed) *Politisk strategi i firserne*, Copenhagen: Aurora.

Laclau, E. (1992) 'Universalism, particularism, and question of identity', *October*, no 61, pp 83-90.

Laclau, E. (1993a) 'Power and representation', in M. Poster (ed) *Politics, theory and contemporary culture*, New York, NY: Columbia University Press.

Laclau, E. (1993b) 'Discourse', in R.E. Goodin and P. Pettit (eds) *A companion to contemporary political philosophy*, Oxford: Blackwell.

Laclau, E. (1996a) *Emancipation(s)*, London: Verso.

Laclau, E. (1996b) 'Deconstruction, pragmatism, hegemony', in C. Mouffe (ed) *Deconstruction and pragmatism*, London: Routledge.

Laclau, E. and Mouffe, C. (1985) *Hegemony and socialist strategy*, London: Verso.

Lévi-Strauss, C. (1996) *The savage mind*, Oxford: Oxford University Press.

Luhmann, N. (1982) 'World–time and system history', in N. Luhmann, *The differentiation of society*, New York, NY: Columbia University Press.

Luhmann, N. (1985) 'Complexity and meaning', in I. Prigogine, M. Zeleny and E. Morin (eds) *The science and praxis of complexity: Contributions to the symposium held at Montpellier, France, May 9-11, 1984*, Tokyo: United Nations University.

Luhmann, N. (1986a) 'The theory of social systems and its epistemology: reply to Danilo Zolo's critical comments', *Philosophy and Social Science*, vol 16, pp 129-34.

Luhmann, N. (1986b) 'Kunstens medie', in N. Luhmann, *Iagttagelse og paradoks*, Copenhagen: Gyldendal.

Luhmann, N. (1988a) *Erkenntnis als Konstruktion*, Bern: Benteli Verlag.

Luhmann, N. (1988b) 'Frauen, Männer und George Spencer-Brown', *Zeitschrift für Soziologie*, vol 17, no 1, pp 47-117.

Luhmann, N. (1990a) 'The paradox of system differentiation and the evolution of society' in J. Alexander and P. Colomy (eds) *Differentiation theory and social change*, New York, NY: Columbia University Press.

Luhmann, N. (1990b) *Essays on self-reference*, New York, NY: Columbia University Press.

Luhmann, N. (1990c) 'The cognitive program of constructivism and a reality that remains unknown', in W. Krohn, G. Küppers and H. Nowotny (eds) *Selforganization: Portrait of a scientific revolution*, New York, NY: Kluwer Academic Publishers.

Luhmann, N. (1990d) 'Risiko und Gefahr', in N. Luhmann, *Soziologische Aufklarung 5*, Wiesbaden: Westdeutsche Verlag.

Luhmann, N. (1991) 'Am Ende der kritischen Soziologie', *Zeitschrift für Soziologie*, vol 20, pp 147-52.

Luhmann, N. (1993a) *Risk: A sociological theory*, New York, NY: Walter de Gruyter.

Luhmann, N. (1993b) 'Deconstruction as second-order observing', *New Literary History*, vol 24, pp 763-82.

Luhmann, N. (1993c) *Gesellschaftstruktur und Semantik Band – Studien zur Wissenssoziologie der moderne Gesellschaft 3*, Frankfurt am Main: Suhrkamp.

Luhmann, N. (1994a) '"What is the case?" and "What lies behind it": the two sociologies and the theory of society', *Sociological Theory*, vol 12, no 2, pp 126-39.

Luhmann, N. (1994b) 'Speaking and silence', *New German Critique*, vol 61, pp 25-37.

Luhmann, N. (1995a) 'The paradoxy of observing system', *Cultural Critique*, no 31, pp 37-55.

Luhmann, N. (1995b) 'Subjektets nykker og spørgsmålet om mennesket', in J.C. Jacobsen (ed) *Autopoiesis II*, Copenhagen: Politisk Revy, p 46.

Luhmann, N. (1995c) *Social systems*, Stanford, CA: Stanford University Press.

Luhmann, N. (1996) 'On the scientific context of the concept of communication', *Social Science Information*.

Macey, D. (1988) *Lacan in context*, London: Verso.

Mahon, M. (1992) *Foucault's Nietzschean genealogy*, Albany, NY: State University of New York Press.

Megill, A. (1979) 'Foucault, structuralism, and the end of history', *Journal of Modern History*, vol 51, no 3, pp 451-503.

Nietzsche, F. (1988) *On the advantage and disadvantage of history for life*, Indianapolis, IL: Hackett Publishing.

Nietzsche, F. (1998) *On the genealogy of morality*, Indianapolis, IL: Hackett Publishing.

Noujain, E.G. (1987) 'History as genealogy: an exploration of Foucault's approach to history', in A.P. Griffiths (ed) *Contemporary French philosophy*, New York, NY: Cambridge University Press, pp 157-74.

Pedersen, O.K. (1983) *Videnskabsproblemet*, Copenhagen: Aurora.

Pocock, J.G.A. (1987) 'The concepts of a language and the métier d'historien: some considerations on practice', in A. Pagden (ed) *The languages of political theory in early-modern Europe*, Cambridge: Cambridge University Press.

Raffnsøe, S. (1999) 'Historie- eller diskursanalyse? En introduction til Foucault *Les mots et les choses* og *L'archéologie du savoir*', *COS-report 4/99*, Copenhagen: Copenhagen Business School.

Raffnsøe, S. (2000) 'Michel Foucault's dispositionelle magtanalytik', *Grus*.

Regnault, F. (1983) 'Hvad er et epistemologisk brud?', in S.G. Olesen (ed) *Epistemologi*, Copenhagen: Rhodos.

Richter, M. (1990) 'Reconstructing the history of political languages: Pocock, Skinner, and the geschichtliche Grundbegriffe', *History and Theory*, vol 29, pp 38-70.

Richter, M. (1995) *The history of political and social concepts*, New York, NY: Oxford University Press.

Rose, N. (1996) *Intenting ourselves: Psychology, power and personhood*, Cambridge: Cambridge University Press.

Roth, M.S. (1981) 'Foucault's "History of the present"', *History and Theory*, vol 20, pp 32-46.

Röttgers, K. (1982) 'Kritik', in O. Brunner, W. Conze and R. Kosseleck (eds) *Geschichtliche Grundbegriffe, Historisches Lexikon zur politisch-sozialen Sprache in Deutschland, Vol III*, Stuttgart: Klett-Cotta.

Scharff, R. (1974) 'Nietzsche and the "use" of history', *Man and World, An International Philosophical Review*, vol 7, p 74.

Schmidt, L.H. (1990) *Det sociale selv*, Århus: Århus Universitetsforlag.

Schmidt, L.H. and Kristensen J.E. (eds) (1985) *Foucaults Blik*, Århus: Modtryk.

Shiner, L. (1982) 'Reading Foucault: anti-method and the genealogy of power–knowledge', *History and Theory*, vol 21, pp 382-98.

Skinner, Q. (1987) *Machiavelli*, Oxford: Oxford University Press.

Spencer-Brown, G. (1969) *Laws of gorm*, London: George Allen & Unwin.

Stahäli, U. (1998) 'Die Nachträglichkeit der Semantik zum Verhältnis von Sozialstruktur und Semantik', *Soziale Systeme, Zeitschrift für soziologische Theorie*, no 2, pp 315-40.

Stråht, B. (ed) (1990) *Language and the construction of class identity*, Göteborg: Department of History, Göteborg University.

Tully, J. (1988) *Meaning and context: Quentin Skinner and his critics*, London: Polity Press.

von Foerster, J. (1981) *Observing systems*, Seaside, CA: Intersystems Publication.

Appendix A: Examples of other analytical strategies

Analytical strategy	Guiding distinction	Question	Goal of the analysis
Pierre Bourdieu Field analysis	Community/disagreement	How are fields created as communities of disagreement and how do they distribute a network of relative subject positions?	To demonstrate the correlation between history, practice and power
Analysis of communicative competence	Authorising/speech position	How are individuals authorised by institutions so that they not only speak from a position of meaning but also with weight? How can individuals collect social and cultural capital that they can actualise communicatively in specific fields?	
Jürgen Habermas Discourse analysis	Discursive practice/ethics of discourse	In what way does practice deviate from the ethics of discourse?	Emancipation and discourse-ethical communication
Bruno Latour Translation analysis	Translation/association	How are ideas, technologies, and practices propagated by being associated with other ideas, technologies, and practices etc, so that they form a network? In what way does propagation through association simultaneously mean a translation of the propagated phenomena so that phenomena constantly change character and value through their propagation?	To demonstrate the growth of power through distribution and practice in a network
Louis Althusser Symptomatic reading	The invisible in the visible	Which questions are posed by the text? Which answers does the text offer to the questions it poses? Which questions does the text pose without answering them? Which answers does the text offer to questions it does not pose? In sum, what is the prohibited and displaced question that guides and regulates the text and its visibility?	To analyse the imaginary order which regulates people's relationship to their condition of existence with a view to politicisation

Appendix B: Further reading

Examples of empirical analyses in the spirit of Foucault, Koselleck, Laclau and Luhmann

Foucault inspired analysis

Amariglio, J. (1990) 'Economics as postmodern discourse', in W.J. Samuels (ed) *Economics as discourse*, London: Kluwer.

Barnes, T.J. and Duncan, J.S. (1992) *Writing worlds: Discourse, text and metaphor in the representation of landscape*, London: Routledge.

Chiapello, E. and Fairclough, N. (2002) 'Understanding the new management ideology: a transdisciplinary contribution from critical discourse analysis and new sociology of capitalism', *Discourse & Society*, vol 13, no 2, pp 185-208.

Cruikshank, B. (1999) *The will to empower*, Ithaca, NJ: Cornell University Press.

Dean, M. (1992) 'A genealogy of the government of poverty', *Economy & Society*, vol 21, no 3, pp 215-51.

Dean, M. (1994) '"A social structure of many souls": moral regulation, government and self-formation', *Canadian Journal of Sociology*, vol 10, no 2, pp 145-68.

Dean, M. (1995) 'Governing the unemployed self in an active society', *Economy & Society*, vol 24, no 4, pp 559-83.

Dean, M. (1998) 'Administrating asceticism, reworking the ethical life of the unemployed citizen', in M. Dean and B. Hindess (ed) *Governing Australia*, Cambridge: Cambridge University Press.

Donzelot, J. (1988) 'The promotion of the social', *History of the Present*, vol 3, pp 5-15.

Donzelot, J. (1997) *The policing of families*, Baltimore, MD: Johns Hopkins University Press.

Eder, K. (1996) *The social construction of nature*, London: Sage Publications.

Farmer, J. (1995) *The language of public administration*, University of Alabama Press.

Foucault, M. (ed) (1982) *Pierre Riviere, having slaughtered my mother, my sister, and my brother*, London: University of Nebraska Press.

Foucault, M. (1974) *The order of things: An archaeology of the human sciences*, London: Routledge.

Foucault, M. (1976): *The birth of the clinic: An archaeology of medical perception*, London: Routledge.

Foucault, M. (1987) *Mental illness and psychology*, Berkeley, CA: University of California Press.

Foucault, M. (1988) *The history of sexuality Vol 2: The use of pleasure*, Harmondsworth: Penguin.

Foucault, M. (1990) *The history of sexuality Vol 3: The care of the self*, Harmondsworth: Penguin.

Foucault, M. (1991) *Discipline and punish*, Harmondsworth: Penguin.

Foucault, M. (1998) *The history of sexuality Vol 1: The will to knowledge*, Harmondsworth: Penguin.

Foucault, M. (2001) *Madness and civilization*, London: Routledge.

Hacking, I. (1986) 'Making up people', in T.C. Heller, M. Sosna and D.E. Wellbery (eds) *Reconstructing individualism*, Stanford, CA: Stanford University Press.

Hoskin, K. (1992) 'Control, organization, and accounting: a genealogy of modern knowledge-power', *System Practice*, vol 5, no 4, pp 425-39.

Laqueur, T. (1994) *Making sex*, Harvard, MA: Harvard University Press.

Lemke, L.J. (1995) *Textual politics: Discourse and social dynamics*, London: Taylor & Francis.

Lupton, D. (1995) *The imperative of health-public health and the regulated body*, London: Sage Publications.

Miller, P. and Napier, C. (1993) 'Genealogies of calculation', *Accounting, Organizations and Society*, vol 18, nos 7/8, pp 631-47.

Miller, P. and O'Leary, T. (1987) 'Accounting and the construction of the governable person', *Accounting, Organizations and Society*, vol 12, no 3, pp 235-65.

Miller, P. and Rose, N. (1990) 'Governing economic life', *Economy & Society*, vol 19, no 1, pp 1-31.

Miller, P. and Rose, N. (1995) 'Production, identity, and democracy', *Theory and Society*, vol 24, no 4, pp 427-67.

Mitchell, T. (1988) *Colonising Egypt*, Cambridge: Cambridge University Press.

Novas, C. and Rose, N. (2000) 'Genetic risk and the birth of the somatic individual', *Economy & Society*, vol 29, no 4, pp 485-513.

Rose, N. (1985) *The psychological complex: Psychology, politics and society in England 1869-1939*, London: Routledge and Kegan Paul.

Wodak, R. (1996) *Disorders of discourse*, London: Longman.

Laclau inspired analysis

Cornell, D., Rosenfeld, M. and Carlson, D.G. (eds) (1992) *Deconstruction and the possibility of justice*, New York, NY: Routledge.

Dalton, C. (1985) 'An essay in the deconstruction of contract doctrine', *The Yale Law Journal*, vol 94, no 5, pp 999-1113.

Daly, G. (1991) 'The discursive construction of economic space: logics of organization and disorganization', *Economy & Society*, vol 20, no 1, pp 79-102.

Howarth, D. and Norval, A. (eds) (1998) *South Africa in transition*, London: Macmillan.

Howarth, D., Norval, A.J. and Stavrakakis, Y. (2000) *Discourse theory and political analysis: Identities, hegemonies and social change*, Manchester: Manchester University Press.

Norval, A.J. (1996) *Deconstructing apartheid discourse*, London: Verso.

Smith, A.M. (1994) *New right discourse on race and sexuality: Britain, 1968-1990*, Cambridge: Cambridge University Press.

Smith, A.M. (1998) *Laclau and Mouffe: The radical democratic imaginary*, New York, NY: Routledge.

Luhmann inspired analysis

Andersen, N.Å. (2000) 'Public market – political firms', *Acta Sociologica*, no 1.

Andersen, N.Å. and Born, A. (2000) 'Complexity and change: two "semantic tricks" in the triumphant oscillating organization', *System Practice and Action Research*, vol 13, no 3.

Baecker, D. (ed) (1999) *Problems of form*, Stanford, CA: Stanford University Press.

Baecker, D. (1992) 'The writing of accounting', *Stanford Literature Review*, vol 9, no 2, pp 157-78.

Graham, P. (1999) 'Critical system theory', *Communications Research*, vol 26, no 4, pp 482-507.

Hernes, T. and Bakken, T. (ed) (2000) *Niklas Luhmann's autopoiesis and organization theory*, Copenhagen: Copenhagen Business School Press.

Jessop, B., Brenner, N., Jones, M. and Macleod, G. (eds) (2002) *State/space*, Oxford: Blackwell.

Luhmann, N. (1989) *Ecological communication*, Oxford: Polity Press.

Luhmann, N. (1990) *Political theory in the welfare state*, Berlin: Walter de Gruyter.

Luhmann, N. (1993) *Risk: A sociological theory*, Berlin: Walter de Gruyter.

Luhmann, N. (1998) *Love as passion: The codification of intimacy*, Stanford, CA: Stanford University Press.

Luhmann, N. (2000) *Art as a social system (Meridian: crossing aesthetics)*, Stanford, CA: Stanford University Press.

Luhmann, N. (2000) *The reality of the mass media*, Oxford: Polity Press.

Paterson, J. and Teubner, G. (1998) 'Changing maps: empirical legal autopoiesis', *Social and Legal Studies*, vol 7, no 4, pp 451-86.

Stichweh, R. (1990) 'Self-organization and autopoiesis in the development of modern science', in W. Krohn, G. Küppers and H. Nowotny (eds) *Selforganization: Portrait of a scientific revolution*, London: Kluwer.

Stichweh, R. (1996) 'Science in the system of world society', *Social Science Information*, vol 35, no 2, pp 327-40.

Stichweh, R. (1997) 'The stranger – on the sociology of indifference', *Thesis Eleven*, no 51, pp 1-16.

Teubner, G. (ed) (1997) *Global law without a state*, Aldershot: Dartmouth.

Teubner, G. (1986) 'After legal instrumentalism? Strategic models of post-regulatory law', in G. Teubner (ed) *Dilemmas of law in the welfare state*, New York, NY: Walter de Gruyter.

Teubner, G. (1993) 'Piercing the contractual veil? The social responsibility of contractual networks', in T. Wilhelmsson (ed) *Perspectives of critical contract law*, Aldershot: Dartmouth.

Teubner, G. (1993) *Law as an autopoietic system*, Oxford: Blackwell.

Teubner, G. (1998) 'After privatisation', *Current Legal Problems*, vol 51, pp 393-424.

Teubner, G., Farmer, L. and Murphy, D. (eds) (1994) *Environmental law and ecological responsibility: The concept of practice of ecological self-organization*, London: John Wiley & Sons.

Weiss, G. (2000) 'A difference that makes no difference? Decision-making on employment in European Parliament', in P. Muntigl, G. Weiss and R. Wodak (eds) *European Union discourses on un/employment*, Amsterdam: John Benjamins Publishing.

Wodak, R. (2000) 'From conflict to consensus?', in P. Muntigl, G. Weiss and R. Wodak (eds) *European Union discourses on un/employment*, Amsterdam: John Benjamins Publishing.

Koselleck inspired analysis

Ball, T. and Pocock, J.G.A. (eds) (1988) *Conceptual change and the constitution*, Lawrence, KA: University Press of Kansas.

Ball, T. (1988) *Transforming political discourse: Political theory and critical conceptual history*, Oxford: Basil Blackwell.

Knemeyer, F.-L. (1980) 'Polizei', *Economy & Society*, vol 9, no 2, pp 173-96.

Koselleck, R. and Presner, T.S. (2002) *Practice of conceptual history: Timing history spacint concepts*, Cultural Memory in the Present, Stanford, CA: Stanford University Press.

Koselleck, R. (1985) *Futures past*, Cambridge, MA: MIT Press.

Koselleck, R. (1988) *Critique and crisis*, Oxford: Berg.

Walther, R. (1989) 'Economic liberalism', *Economy & Society*, vol 13, pp 178-207.

INDEX

A

'actuality and potentiality'
(Luhmann) 12, 73
Althusser, L. 2, 3, 49, 52, 125
analytical strategies
    Anderson's views 93-118, 117*fig*
    definition XIII, 93-6
    methodological issues XIII-XV
    ee also strategy types under Foucault;
        Koselleck; Laclau; Luhmann
Anderson, N. A. XIX-XXII, 93-118
apparatus (dispositif) (Foucault)
    27-30, 28*fig*, 29*fig*, 31*tab*, 97*tab*,
    99, 106-7, 114*tab*
    see also archaeology; genealogy;
        technologies of the self
archaeology (Foucault) 8-16, 31*tab*,
    97*tab*, 98, 105
    ee also apparatus; genealogy;
        technologies of the self
Archaeology of knowledge (Foucault) 8,
    17
'articulation' (Laclau) 50, 51

B

Balibar, E. 2, 24
Barthes, R. 6
'before and after' (Koselleck) 44
Beronius, M. 20
    Between facts and norms (Habermas)
    XVIII
    Birth of the clinic (Foucault) 105
Born, A. XXI, 115
Bourdieu, P. XVIII, 125
Brenner, N. 27, 30
Brunner, J. 33

C

Chouliaraki, L. XIX
'communication' (Luhmann) 74-7

'concepts and counter-concepts'
    (Koselleck) VI, 33-48, 47*fig*,
    48*tab*, 99-100
'condensed meaning' (Luhmann) *see*
    'meaning and condensed
    meaning'
counter-concepts (Koselleck) *see*
    'concepts and counter concepts'

D

Davidson, A.I. 25
de Saussure, F. 3, 6, 52
Dean, M. 27
deconstructivist analysis (Laclau)
    56-61, 62*tab*, 97*tab*, 100, 110,
    114*tab*
    relationship with discourse analysis
    58-9, 58*fig*
    see also hegemonic analysis
Deleuze, G. 27
Derrida, J. 49-50, 51
    Of grammatology 57
Descombes, V. 4-5
diachronic and synchronous analysis
    (Koselleck) 35, 43, 47*fig*
'difference' (Laclau) *see* 'equivalence
    and difference'
'difference' (Luhmann) *see* 'form and
    difference', 'unity and difference'
differentiation analysis (Luhmann)
    81-3, 83*tab*, 89-90, 90*fig*, 92*tab*,
    97*tab*, 102, 111, 114*tab*
    see also form analysis; formation
    analysis; media analysis; semantic
    analysis; systems analysis
Discipline and punish (Foucault) 6-7,
    19, 27
discourse and discoursivity
    Foucault VI
    Laclau VI, 50-4, 72, 100
discourse analysis
    (Foucault) 1-32, 114*tab*

relationship with deconstructive analysis (Laclau) 58-9

discourse theory
and Laclau 12, 49-62
comparison with systems theory 93-7

discoursivity *see* discourse and discoursivity

'discursive points' (Laclau) *see* 'nodal points'

dispositive (Foucault) *see* apparatus

'dissimilarity' (Luhmann) see 'similarity and dissimilarity'

'distinction' (Luhmann) *see* 'indication and distinction'

E

'empty-signifier' (Laclau) 54, 109
see also 'floating signifier', 'signs and signifiers'

'environment' (Luhmann) *see* 'system and environment'

'equivalence and difference' (Laclau) 55*fig*

Esposito, E. 69

F

Fairclough, N. XVIII, XIX

first order observation (Luhmann) *see* observation

'floating signifier' (Lacan) 53, 109
Laclau's views 53-4
see also 'empty signifier'; 'signs and signifiers'

form analysis (Luhmann) 64, 78-80, 88-9, 89*fig*, 92*tab*, 97*tab*, 101, 110-111, 114*tab*
see also differentiation analysis; formation analysis; media analysis; semantic analysis; systems analysis

'form and difference' (Luhmann) VI, 64, 65*fig*

'form and medium' (Luhmann) 97*tab*, 114*tab*

formation analysis (Luhmann) 97*tab*, 114*tab*
see also differentiation analysis; form analysis; media analysis; semantic analysis; systems analysis

Foucault, M. 1-32, 36, 49, 63, 86
analysis of statements 10-16
analysis of structuralism 6
apparatus (dispositif) 27-30, 28*fig*, 29*fig*, 31*tab*, 97*tab*, 99, 106-7, 114*tab*
archaeology 8-16, *31tab*, 97*tab*, 98, 105
Archaeology of knowledge 8, 17
as discourse analyst 2-3
as structuralist 2-3
Birth of the clinic 105
Discipline and punish 6-7, 19, 27
discourse analysis 1-32, 114*tab*
discourse and discoursivity VI
genealogy 17-23, 21*fig*, *31tab*, 97*tab*, 98, 105-6, 114*tab*
History of sexuality 27
Madness and civilization 3, 4, 19
'madness and reason' 3-6
Mental illness and psychology 5-6
on prison as punishment/cure 6-7
on punishment 6-7, 19
Order of things 6
Panopticon 7
technologies of the self 24-6, 26*fig*, *31tab*, 97*tab*, 99, 106, 114*tab*

G

genealogy (Foucault) 17-23, 21*fig*, *31tab*, 97*tab*, 99, 105-6, 114*tab*
see also apparatus; archaeology; technologies of the self

'generality and singularity' (Koselleck) 39-41, 47*fig*

Gramsci, A. 49

Günther, G. 64

H

Habermas, J. XII, 125

Between facts and norms XVIII
Knowledge and human interest XVIII
Hacking, I. 25
hegemonic analysis (Laclau) 49, 55-
    6, 59, 62, *62tab*, 97*tab*, 100, 108-
    9, 114*tab*
    see also deconstructivist analysis
Hegemony and socialist strategy
    (Laclau) 49
Heidegger, M. 43, 45
history *see* genealogy
history of concepts (Koselleck)
    33-48, *48tab*, 97*tab*, 99, 107-8,
    114*tab*
    see also semantic field analysis
History of sexuality (Foucault) 27

I

Ifversen, J. 13, 16, 33, 34, 35, 38
'indication and distinction'
    (Luhmann) 65-7
insanity *see* madness and reason
'inside and outside' (Koselleck)
    44-5, 47*fig*

K

Kaufmann, L.H. 68
Kent, C.A. 32
Kneer, G. 75
Knowledge and human interest
    (Habermas) XVIII
knowledge archaeology (Foucault)
    see archaeology
Koselleck, R. XVII, 33-48, 87, 88
    'before and after' 44
    'concepts and counter-concepts'
    VI, 33-48, 47*fig*, 48*tab*, 99-100
    diachronic and synchronous
    analysis 35, 43, 47*fig*
    'generality and singularity' 39-41,
    47*fig*
    history of concepts 33-48, *48tab*,
    97*tab*, 99, 107-8, 114*tab*
    'inside and outside' 44-5, 47*fig*

semantic field analysis 38-47,
    48*tab*, 97*tab*, 99-100, 108, 114*tab*
    'up and down' 45, 47*fig*
Krause, D. 64
Krause-Jensen, E. 7
Kristensen XVII, 2
Kristeva, J. 6

L

Lacan, J. 49, 53, 54
    'floating signifier' 53, 109
Laclau, E. XVII, 1, 36, 37, 39,
    49-62, 63, 72, 74, 78
        'articulation' 50, 51
        deconstructivist analysis
        56-61, *62tab*, 97*tab*, 100, 110,
        114*tab*
        relationship with discourse
        analysis 58-9
    discourse and discoursivity 50-4,
        72, 100
    discourse theory 12, 49-62
    'empty signifier' 54, 109
    'equivalence and difference' 55*fig*
    hegemonic analysis 49, 55-6, 59,
        62, *62tab*, 97*tab*, 100, 108-9,
        114*tab*
    Hegemony and socialist strategy 49
    'logics' 59-61
    'nodal points' VII, 51
    views on Lacan's 'floating signifier'
        53-4
Latour, B. 125
Levi-Strauss, C. 3, 6, 53
'logics' (Laclau) 59-61
Luhmann, N. XV, XVII, 1, 50,
    63-93, 93
    'actuality and potentiality' 12, 73
    'communication' 74-7
    differentiation analysis 81-3, *83tab*,
        89-90, 90*fig*, *92tab*, 97*tab*, 102,
        111, 114*tab*
    form analysis 64, 78-80, 88-9,
        89*fig*, *92tab*, 97*tab*, 101, 110-111,
        114*tab*

'form and difference' VI, 64, 65*fig*
'form and medium' 97*tab*, 114*tab*
formation analysis 97*tab*, 114*tab*
'indication and distinction' 65-7
'meaning and condensed meaning'
   12, 72-4, 86, 87, 102
media analysis 83-6, 84*fig*, 86*fig*,
   90-1, 91*fig*, 92*tab*, 97*tab*, 103, 112
'media and form' 83-6, 84*fig*, 86*fig*,
   97*tab*, 103, 112
observation VII, 64-71, 71*tab*,
   77-8, 93-5
semantic analysis 86-90, 89*fig*,
   90*fig*, 92*tab*, 97*tab*, 102, 112-3,
   114*tab*
'similarity and dissimilarity' 82,
   92*tab*, 97*tab*, 102
'system and environment' 66, 67*fig*,
   69, 80-1, 81*fig*, 101
systems analysis 82-3, 90-1, 91*fig*,
   92*tab*, 97*tab*, 101, 111
systems theory 12, 63-92
'unity and difference' 78-9, 101

M

Macey, D. 53
Madness and civilization (Foucault) 3,
   4, 19
'madness and reason' (Foucault) 3-6
Mahon, M. 32
'meaning and condensed
   meaning' (Luhmann) 12, 72-4,
   86, 87, 102
media analysis (Luhmann) 83-6,
   84*fig*, 86*fig*, 90-1, 91*fig*, 92*tab*,
   97*tab*, 103, 112
   see also differentiation analysis;
   form analysis; formation analysis;
   semantic analysis; systems analysis
'media and form' (Luhmann) 83-6,
   84*fig*, 86*fig*, 97*tab*, 103, 112
'medium' (Luhmann) *see* 'form and
   medium'
Megill, A. 19, 32

mental illness *see* 'madness and
   reason'
Mental illness and psychology
   (Foucault) 5-6
Mouffe, C. 49, 50, 51, 56, 61

N

Nassehi, A. 75
Nietzsche, F. 17-18
'nodal points' (Laclau) VII, 51

O

observation (Luhmann) VII, 64-71,
   71*tab*, 77-8, 93-5
Of grammatology (Derrida) 57
On the genealogy of morality
   (Nietzsche) 17
Order of things (Foucault) 6
Østergård, U. 34

P

Panopticon (Foucault) 7
Parsons, T. 63
Pedersen, O.K. XI, XII
Pocock, J.G.A. 33
poststructuralism *see* structuralism
'potentiality' (Luhmann) *see*
   'actuality and potentiality'
prison as punishment/cure
   (Foucault) 6-7
punishment (Foucault) 6-7, 19

R

Raffnsøe, S. 28, 32
'reason' (Foucault) *see* 'madness and
   reason'
Regnault, F. XV
Richter, M. 33
Roth, M.S. 32

S

Scharff, R. 18
Schmidt, L.H. XVII, 2, 24
second order observation
   (Luhmann) *see* observation

self-technology (Foucault) *see* technologies of the self

semantic analysis (Luhmann) 86-90, 89*fig*, 90*fig*, 92*tab*, 97*tab*, 102, 112-3, 114*tab*

see also differentiation analysis; form analysis; formation analysis; media analysis; systems analysis

semantic field analysis (Koselleck) 38-47, 48*tab*, 97*tab*, 99-100, 108, 114*tab*

see also history of concepts

Shiner, L. 32

Simmel, G. 24

'signs and signifiers' (de Saussure) 52-3

see also 'empty signifier'; 'floating signifier'

'similarity and dissimilarity' 82, 92*tab*, 97*tab*, 102

'singularity' (Koselleck) *see* 'generality and singularity'

Skinner, Q. 33-4

Spencer-Brown, C. 63, 64-5, 84

statements VII

Foucault's analysis 10-16

Stråht, B. 33

structuralism 2-3, 6

synchronous analysis (Koselleck) *see* diachronic and synchronous analysis

'system and environment' (Luhmann) 66, 67*fig*, 69, 80-1, 81*fig*, 101

systems analysis (Luhmann) 82-3, 90-1, 91*fig*, 93*fig*, 92*tab*, 97*tab*, 101, 111

see also differentiation analysis; form analysis; formation analysis; media analysis; semantic analysis

systems theory (Luhmann) 12, 63-92

comparison with discourse theory 93-7

T

technologies of the self (Foucault) 24-6, 26*fig*, 31*tab*, 97*tab*, 99, 106, 114*tab*

see also apparatus; archaeology; genealogy

Time and being (Heidegger) 43

Tully, J. 33

U

'unity and difference' (Luhmann) 78-9, 101

'up and down' (Koselleck) 45, 47*fig*

V

von Foerster, J. 64

Z

Zizek, S. 49

Understanding welfare: Social issues, policy and practice

Series Editor: Professor Saul Becker, Department of Social Sciences, Loughborough University

NEW <u>definitive</u> textbook series for students of social policy

From The Policy Press and the Social Policy Association

Launching the series in 2003

Understanding social security
Issues for policy and practice

Edited by Jane Millar, University of Bath

There is an urgent need for an up-to-date and critical analysis of changes in policy and practice in this important area of governance. *Understanding social security* provides this analysis in a lively and accessible way. It covers a wide range of policy areas and links policy analysis to analysis of implementation and changing practice.

Paperback £17.99 ISBN 1 86134 419 8
Hardback £50.00 ISBN 1 86134 420 1
240 x 172mm 256 pages TBC July 2003

Understanding the finance of welfare
What welfare costs and how to pay for it

Howard Glennerster, London School of Economics and Political Science

This is a much needed and up-to-date text on a rapidly changing policy field. The author, Howard Glennerster, is the pre-eminent author in the field and this book provides an excellent introduction to the subject. It makes economic theory and the complex funding arrangements that underpin social policy accessible to students across a range of social science disciplines, including social policy, sociology and social work.

Paperback £17.99 ISBN 1 86134 405 8
Hardback £50.00 ISBN 1 86134 406 6
240 x 172mm 256 pages TBC July 2003

Inspection copies

Please order from:
Marston Book Services, PO Box 269,
Abingdon, Oxon, OX14 4YN
Tel: 01235 465538, Fax: 01235 465556
Email: inspections@marston.co.uk

Forthcoming in 2004

Understanding research methods for social policy and practice

Edited by Saul Becker and Alan Bryman, Loughborough University

Understanding social citizenship
Themes and perspectives for policy and practice

Pete Dwyer, University of Leeds

Understanding work-life balance
Policies for a family-friendly Britain

Margaret May, London Guildhall University

Forthcoming in 2005

Understanding immigration and migration policy
Contradictions and continuities

Rosemary Sales, Middlesex University

Forthcoming in 2006

Understanding child welfare interventions
The provision of services for children in need

Harriet Ward, Loughborough University

> *"This exciting new series will be essential reading for students across a range of subjects and courses who need to gain a comprehensive understanding of welfare issues."*
> Pete Alcock, Chair, Social Policy Subject Benchmarking Group

www.policypress.org.uk

Biography and social exclusion in Europe
Experiences and life journeys

Edited by **Prue Chamberlayne**, School of Health and Social Welfare, The Open University, **Michael Rustin**, Faculty of Social Sciences, University of East London and **Tom Wengraf**, School of Social Science, Middlesex University

Throughout Europe, standardised approaches to social policy and practice are being radically questioned and modified. Beginning from the narrative detail of individual lives, this book re-thinks welfare predicaments, emphasising gender, generation, ethnic and class implications of economic and social deregulation.

Based on 250 life-story interviews in seven European Union countries, *Biography and social exclusion in Europe*:

- analyses personal struggles against social exclusion to illuminate local milieus and changing welfare regimes and contexts;
- points to challenging new agendas for European politics and welfare, beyond the rhetoric of communitarianism and the New Deal;
- vividly illustrates the lived experience and environmental complexity working for and against structural processes of social exclusion;
- re-fashions the interpretive tradition as a teaching and research tool linking macro and micro realities.

Students, academic teachers and professional trainers, practitioners, politicians, policy makers and researchers in applied and comparative welfare fields will all benefit from reading this book.

Contents: Introduction: from biography to social policy *Michael Rustin and Prue Chamberlayne*; Suffering the fall of the Berlin wall: blocked journeys in Spain and Germany *William Hungerbühler, Elisabet Tejero and Laura Torrabadella*; Guilty victims: social exclusion in contemporary France *Numa Murard*; Premodernity and postmodernity in Southern Italy *Antonella Spanò*; A tale of class differences in contemporary Britain *Michael Rustin*; The shortest way out of work *Numa Murard*; Male journeys into uncertainty *Elisabeth Ioannidi-Kapolou and Elisabeth Mestheneos*; Love and emancipation *Birgitta Thorsell*; Female identities in late modernity *Antonella Spanò*; Gender and family in the development of Greek state and society *Elisabeth Mestheneos and Elisabeth Ioannidi-Kapolou*; Corporatist structure and cultural diversity in Sweden *Martin Peterson*; 'Migrants': a target-category for social policy? Experiences of first-generation migration *Roswitha Breckner*; Second-generation transcultural lives *Prue Chamberlayne*; Biographical work and agency innovation: relationships, reflexivity and theory-in-use *Tom Wengraf*; Conclusions: social transitions and biographical work *Prue Chamberlayne*.

Paperback £19.99 (US$75.00) ISBN 1 86134 309 4
Hardback £50.00 ISBN 1 86134 310 8
234 x 156mm 352 pages November 2002

Available from:
Marston Book Services, PO Box 269, Abingdon, Oxon OX14 4YN.
Tel: +44 (0)1235 465500 Email: direct.orders@marston.co.uk
Postage and packaging: Please add £2.75 (UK) £3.50 (Europe) £5.00 (Rest of the World)

www.policypress.org.uk

Love, hate and welfare
Psychosocial approaches to policy and practice

Lynn Froggett, Department of Social Work,
University of Central Lancashire

This book presents a psychosocial examination of the changing relationships between users of services, professionals and managers in the post-war welfare state. It challenges the current emphasis on consumer rights by linking social responsibility to its psychosocial roots and breaks new ground in theorising the links between the intimate day-to-day experiences of care and the development of social policy.

Love, hate and welfare:

- characterises psychosocial dimensions of social citizenship, consumerism, partnerships and active welfare;
- develops practice-based perspectives on changing social relations of care;
- discusses the psychic dimensions of entitlement, risk, responsibility, compassion and dependency in the welfare system;
- develops a grid to link the interpersonal, institutional and sociopolitical dimensions of successive post-war welfare settlements;
- explores the potential contribution of psychoanalytic concepts to social policy and practice.

This book is aimed at all those who have an interest in the development of responsive welfare institutions, including policy makers, professionals and academics.

Contents: Introduction; *Part One:* Between fracture and solidarity: Psychosocial welfare; Old welfare: from warriors to citizens; No welfare: privatisation of concern; Mixed welfare: consumption and compassion; *Part Two:* Compassion, recognition and ethics of care; Recognition, practice and the organisation; The political environment; Vision, voice and story.

Paperback £17.99 (US$28.95) ISBN 1 86134 343 4
Hardback £45.00 (US$69.95) ISBN 1 86134 344 2
234 x 156mm 216 pages October 2002

Available from:
Marston Book Services, PO Box 269, Abingdon, Oxon OX14 4YN.
Tel: +44 (0)1235 465500 Email: direct.orders@marston.co.uk
Postage and packaging: Please add £2.75 (UK) £3.50 (Europe)
£5.00 (Rest of the World)

www.policypress.org.uk